I0003231

A Philosophy
for
Information Technology

Theodore F Corsaro

A Philosophy for Information Technology
By Theodore F Corsaro

Copyright © 2013 submitted to eco.copyright.gov

Cover Art by Kip Ayers

© Theodore F. Corsaro, 2013. Unauthorized use and/or duplication of this material without express and written permission from this author and/or owner is strictly prohibited. Excerpts and links may be used, provided that full and clear credit is given to Theodore F. Corsaro with appropriate and specific direction to the original content.

ISBN: 1489588000
ISBN-13: 9781489588005

Contents

List of Figures and Tables

Figures

Tables

Dedication

————⟪⟫————

To my wife, Judi, who has listened to me talk, think aloud for many years, and has always told me to just do it.

To my daughters, Jessica and Alexandra, who never could explain what I do for a living but always thought writing was a good idea.

Preface

━━━ ◆◆◆◆◆◆◆◆◆◆◆◆◆◆ ━━━

In college, I was a business major with a focus in accounting. I had read the projections that accounting and business were where the jobs would be in the years to come, and I was proficient in math. Like most college students, where I started was very different from where I landed. The valuable aspect to accounting is that it is the nuts-and-bolts of business; the downside is that it could not maintain my interest. I also took some computer science courses because they interested me. The blending of information technology and accounting had not yet penetrated the college curricula, and I was a fish out of water when I took these classes, but they left a lasting impression that would lead me to my next career.

After working at a health care company, a nonprofit organization, and an engineering firm, I decided that I would take Pascal classes at night school because I was finding that accounting was just boring me.[1] As fate would have it, Pascal turned out to be one of best computer language choices I could have selected. It was structured, and it presented disciplined methods of programming that would stay with me. I was an assistant controller at an engineering firm when my brother introduced me to a computer consultant, Cy Radford, who was working at his commodity trading firm. It was truly fortuitous for two reasons: he was looking for someone with a business background who had an interest in learning coding, and he was very good at what he did. It is unlikely that I would have moved from accounting into software consulting without someone who valued my business background more than my limited knowledge of computer programming.

Cy worked in a somewhat obscure programming environment called Pick.[2] Learning the concepts and structure of Pick was a great learning experience, and it imparted knowledge that I still leverage today. I was fortunate that Pick had penetrated a large number of vertical business markets,[3] and I thus was exposed to distributors, legal firms, commodity traders, drug store chains, and educators. I gained an invaluable set of experiences I would draw on throughout my professional career. Being able to speak with chief financial officers, chief executive officers, and executors of the tasks that make an organization run taught me the nuances and commonalities of organizations and the linkages among processes, people, and data.

---

1   "Pascal is an influential imperative and procedural programming language, designed in 1968–1969 and published in 1970 by Niklaus Wirth as a small and efficient language intended to encourage good programming practices using structured programming and data structuring." Wikipedia, "Pascal," https://en.wikipedia.org/wiki/Pascal_(programming_language).

2   "The Pick operating system (often called just 'the Pick system' or simply 'Pick') is a demand-paged, multiuser, virtual memory, time-sharing computer operating system based around a unique 'multivalued' database. Pick is used primarily for business data processing. Though its use has never been properly advertised, its capabilities are far ahead of their time and there is still a strong enthusiastic user community." Wikipedia, "Pick operating system," http://en.wikipedia.org/wiki/Pick_operating_system

3   "A vertical market is a market in which vendors offer goods and services specific to an industry, trade, profession, or other group of customers with specialized needs." Wikipedia, "Vertical market," http://en.wikipedia.org/wiki/Vertical_market

The next change in my profession occurred when I took a corporate job in Charleston, South Carolina. We had lived in Boston, which today is still one of my favorite cities, but my wife and I wanted to raise our daughters outside of a large urban environment and wanted to get away from winter. As it turned out, we moved to one the best small cities in America. In Charleston, my corporate job allowed me to work within different areas of the organization. My team developed a distributed field service software package that integrated with a mainframe for billing. We would later collapse the software into a centralized call center and leverage the structure of the software so that limited changes were required. I was able to bring Cy down to integrate paging into our field service application.

Over the years, I would work with various high-level consulting organizations and move into a marketing group that also worked on clinical outcomes. I also worked on an acquisition that was later determined not viable but left me with experience that is still useful to me today. My company also merged into our parent organization, and the politics and anxieties of being acquired could now be added to my work experience. Acquisition was a valuable but disturbing process that impacted my own thoughts when we acquired other organizations and I worked on integrating them within the corporation.

At one point, I was part of a team that was tasked with developing a strategic information technology plan for the organization. After sixteen weeks of work, I wrote my first published article, "What Consultants Bring to the Table" (see appendix 2).[4] This was a catharsis for me, and allowed me to express my views about the pros and cons of working with consultants on internal strategic projects. The article expresses some of the rawer versions of concepts that I flesh out more completely in this book.

I later became a director of knowledge management, a grand title that I tried to explain to my daughters unsuccessfully.

---

4   Theodore F. Corsaro, "What Consultants Bring to the Table," ADVANCE for Health Information Executives, August 1998.

As it turned out, this became one of my favorite professional positions. It was during this time that I became involved with business intelligence software and marketing analysis and published my next two articles, "The Newest Toy Syndrome" and "When the Cooks Don't Know What the Customers Are Ordering."[5] As with my first article, they related my observations about events that take place within an organization when new technology is brought in, and the disconnects that take place between processes and the data created and used by those processes. These articles are also precursors to concepts outlined in this book. At the tail end of these experiences, I became involved in simulation modeling. I viewed this as the logical end result of all the various work I had completed because it took the results of analysis and made the data into something that was predictive and based on algorithms. This lead to my first academic poster presentation, "Measuring the Impact of a Medical Intervention with Simulation Modeling."[6]

It was at this time that executive shuffling and economic pressures set the stage for me to be asked to move to another city and office or to leave the company. I saw no great value in moving, so I left. I then spent time at a biotech start-up as business development manager and then returned to my former company as a consultant to support the very field service system I had developed, while it was being replaced with an enterprise resource planning (ERP) system.[7] I would later be

5   Theodore F. Corsaro, "The Newest Toy Syndrome," *ADVANCE for Health Information Executives,* February 1998; Theodore F. Corsaro, "When the Cooks Don't Know What the Customers are Ordering," *ADVANCE for Health Information Executives,* February 2001.

6   Mark Wolin, Theodore Corsaro, Frank McGuire, Stephanie Amlung, and Kathy L. McClelland, "Measuring the Impact of a Medical Intervention with Simulation Modeling," poster presented at the Annual Meeting of the Association for Health Services Research, Los Angeles, 2000.

7   "Enterprise resource planning (ERP) systems integrate internal and external management information across an entire organization, embracing finance/accounting, manufacturing, sales and service, customer relationship management, etc. ERP systems automate this activity with an integrated software application. Their purpose is to facilitate the flow of information between all business functions inside the boundaries of the organization and manage the connections to outside stakeholders." Wikipedia, "Enterprise resource planning," http://en.wikipedia.org/wiki/Enterprise_resource_planning

rehired and would work more deeply in the business intelligence area with Oracle and SQL. The irony of working with Oracle is that the Pick software I had worked with previously could have become like Oracle if it had been marketed and promoted correctly.

I looked back on all these experiences and lessons as I wrote this book. Working with numerous consultants made me a firm believer in having a philosophy and a methodology when working on information technology projects. Methodologies are inadequate by themselves. There are too many times when a concrete philosophy is required to bridge the gaps of any methodology, and too many times when a process needs the overarching support of a philosophy to be effectively developed. A philosophy provides clarity when the pushes and pulls of projects cloud their true objectives. When time and money drive changes in course, you need a philosophy that will allow you to focus and maintain the core purpose of your activities. In the absence of such a philosophy, there is variability, the lack of a solid foundation on which to build, and this ultimately creates a commodity outcome where there should be competitive advantage. In this book there are examples of what can happen to projects that get lost as they progress and simply defy logic when they are dissected postmortem but appeared to make sense when they were executed. Yes, smart, talented, and determined individuals can have invisible blinders on when completing a technology project that are more effective than those on racehorses.

As you read this book, I hope you feel as I did when reading Burton G. Malkiel's *A Random Walk Down Wall Street*[8] — that is, entertained, wiser, and (in the case of the present volume) believing that you have grasped the fundamental ideas that make information technology projects function. To quote Peter Lynch, "There were hundreds of losers in Magellan's portfolio…. Fortunately, they weren't my biggest positions. This is an important aspect of

---

8   Burton G. Malkiel, *A Random Walk Down Wall Street: The Time-Tested Strategy for Successful Investing* (New York: Norton, 2007).

portfolio management—containing your losses."[9] No one wins all the time, but you can make the losses less painful and move ahead by learning lessons from those losses. I believe that it's good to hope for luck, but you can increase the probability for success by thinking clearly and asking basic questions.

---

9   Peter Lynch with John Rothchild, *Beating the Street* (New York: Simon and Schuster, 1994), 137. Lynch ran the Fidelity Magellan Fund from 1977 to 1990.

The Philosophy Aspect

Success has been associated with many human characteristics. After *luck*, words often associated with success are *belief, vision,* and *brilliance*, among other very positive terms. Somewhere in this mix you will also find *philosophy*. I use this term based on the following definition: "A system of principles for guidance in practical affairs." As with almost all human activities, there is usually one approach to an activity that will more likely lead to a positive outcome. It is also true that a philosophy is easier to follow when positive activities are taking place instead of difficult choices being presented in a time-sensitive manner. In the world of information technology (IT), the latter is more often the case. It is at the junction of business needs, time management, business processes, hardware integration, and software development where a coherent philosophy can provide a consistently repeatable approach that balances the myriad of decisions that must be made over time. This book is about a philosophy of technology that can be followed and articulated in the office or boardrooms of any business. It is not as straightforward as "the truth will set you free" or as complex as "the meaning of truth," but a foundation on which a nontechnical person can communicate to a room full of MIT graduates and establish a common basis of understanding. I have chosen the word *philosophy* not to be pretentious but to clearly indicate that you need something that allows you to "step back" from any situation and take a course of action that is forward thinking, overarching in nature, and practical. Actions that have been determined by following process steps have a high probability of preventing the misunderstandings, errors, and cost and time overruns that are much too common when technology is implemented. If terms like *realistic, logical, pragmatic* or *thoughtful* ring truer for you, insert them where appropriate.

When one of my groups worked on completely rewriting a field service application that was going to be the front end to our billing system, I articulated to my team that there would be no hard-coding of values in our software. Some people call this a rule, but it was a philosophy. I explained that I did not want any hidden business rules that were forgotten over time. I did not want us to be needed when codes used by the business changed or when new products were introduced. I wanted to be working on enhancements and improvements suggested by the business. To achieve this philosophy, the system was designed as a fully table-driven system (see chapter 12). If there were payment terms, there was a table from which terms were selected. If there were products, there was a table that contained the characteristics of those products. If there were business rules, they were implemented by using the tables created and understood by the users of the system. Because no philosophy is perfect, I agreed to have only one place where something could be hard-coded. It was in a piece of code that could be shared by all the code routines written. It could be made to comply with all other code and leveraged by everyone, but was totally self-contained. Others would challenge this approach when time was short or the additional work seemed a burden, but they knew what my answer would be and this was the process we followed. This took some additional time, but avoided massive amounts of work time when processes and business rules changed. There would be no huge requirement to review all system logic, as occurred when the year 2000 came to pass. We would modify what the tables contained or how the logic worked with the tables, or we added new tables. The business understood the functionality of such an approach, and introduced ideas I had never considered but very gladly added. As with some philosophies, the real value of this approach was realized years after the software was introduced and adapted to acquisitions, business changes, and staff changes. The users were knowledgeable of the system, and thus capable of making changes without involving us. In the world of software development, you are successful when your users ask for enhancements rather than corrections to problems. A business moves forward when this occurs rather than the circle of implementing, finding problems, fixing, and repeating.

The Technology Aspect

———— ⟪⟫⟫⟫⟫⟫⟫⟫⟫⟫⟫⟫⟫⟫ ————

Many of us are active consumers of technology or have it thrust upon us at work, in our cars, or in stores that we frequent. The volume and sophistication of technology that consumers have at their disposal is unprecedented and expanding into new areas continuously. It is not surprising that these same consumers, web surfers, spreadsheet users, and word processing users view the implementation of technology at their homes and in the workplace to be an extension of the technology they wield in each technology-filled day of their life. It is true that the majority of those who indulge in technology in their personal life adapt and perceive technology presented at work in a less threatening manner. Yet you have to ask, are these same individuals able to differentiate between personal enjoyment and strategic integration of technology into the business process? An alternate way of asking the question is, can any one of them implement a new paperless solution in the office or at the corporate level? Can management select the correct ERP software package that will actually improve its business and

xx   A Philosophy for Information Technology

make all the positive impacts outlined in the standard vendor and management Microsoft PowerPoint presentations because of their personnel technology experiences? The short answer is yes.

This answer is not due to some innate human ability to integrate iPads seamlessly into the work environment or because management is the best ever hired. It is because every single person can ask very specific questions, elicit very specific answers, and not feel that he or she is obligated to hearing and seeing endless technology acronyms. Implementing technology is a skill that can be done thoughtfully or very, very poorly. Doing it well is a mixture of focus, willingness to ask what many may consider "stupid questions", understanding that change scares many people and there are no longer islands of business processes that can act independently of the other business processes and still expect to somehow not impact them.

We are going to walk down the path of technology implementation and, by the end of our walk, you will be able to execute a technology-based project. If you open a box containing a new coffeemaker and feel that you will not be able to set the clock, you can still implement technology. Until the world is controlled by the Matrix, as portrayed in Larry and Andy Wachowski's movie series of the same name, *people* will be what make technology projects successful or failures. Take all the aspects of any technology implementation—hardware, software, networks, websites, and the other million moving parts of any project—and, at the end of the day, it is always *people* who must connect all the moving parts. As I have implied with the Peter Lynch quote earlier, the first undeniable fact is that no technology project will ever be implemented without problems or critics. It is not a negative point of view or lack of belief in the nature of people that makes this statement true; it is just a realistic assessment of the process. After you reach the final page of this book, you can expect that any problems experienced will be manageable and that the critics will have very little to criticize. After all, if no one criticizes, it must not be that important.

Chapter One

Why can you make a technology implementation work?

My philosophy of information technology has a foundational concept that requires me to define how I view business. A business is a collection of process threads that are followed concurrently and sequentially to generate a result. These threads of processes almost always include technology, and they require that people interact with that technology in various manners and for different reasons. Threads of technology are in all aspects of your business; they represent the processes and nature of your business. You value these threads, but may call them *"sales, customer records, charts of accounts, bills,* or any number of other terms, but they are threads of process and data that bind you and your customer together and your employees to their jobs. Clearly, people are not bound by any shackles of imprisonment but by those processes and technological tools used to execute the daily sustaining activities of any organization.

I am a strong supporter of the approach Michael Hammer has outlined in *Beyond Reengineering* that outlines the process-centered organization.[10] To view business as a process and subset of processes and not a set of functions like sales, accounting, and marketing is very useful when determining the role that technology will or should have within your organization. If you view the software used to manage your accounts receivable as a single-function piece of software that individuals use to report aged receivables and total amounts of receivables, you are not viewing this information through a philosophical technology lens.

An alternate view of accounts receivable is as a tool that indicates how your customers perceive the value you provide to their business process, an indication of how your processes impact the manner in which organizations choose to pay you, and a method of collecting funds for services rendered. Now let's expand the example a bit further. If you only want to see accounts receivable aging reports and are taking actions based on the dates and amounts that are presented on the report, you will have people who execute these actions and collect most of the money owed, and that would be the limit of value provided to your organization. If you view accounts receivable as part of the entire selling process, you will have people collecting the money owed but also finding out why customers take sixty days to pay instead of thirty. You will have people trending when payments come in over a thirteen-month time line — for each customer — and spending time trying to glean insight from these data. This information, along with other information from the selling process, may tell you that your product is not considered as valuable as other products purchased for your customers' processes or that you just have not asked them to pay faster or provided incentives that they might value.

I am raising the process (normally considered a function) of accounts receivable to a higher level of relevance within the

---

10   Michael Hammer, *Beyond Reengineering: How the Process-Centered Organization Is Changing Our Work and Our Lives* (New York: Harper Business, 1997).

organization and expecting management to spend time and re-sources understanding what strategic information can be derived and utilized. It is also important to understand that I am raising the importance of the role of accounts receivable *technology*—the individuals who support and work within the area of accounts receivable. This elevation of individuals is intentional, and moves this process out of the mundane and into a strategic realm. Another way to articulate the concept would be, "There are no small parts, only small actors."

Unless your business is purely cash based, you use technol-ogy to record and collect the money owed by your customers and have an opportunity to record information about how and why your customers pay or do not pay you in an expected man-ner. Notice I said "expected manner" and not "timely manner." Again, I am making an argument for viewing accounts receivable as a process that is strategic and heavily technology based and capable of providing tremendous amounts of insight about your business and the business of your customers. Having helped col-lect accounts receivable money, I know that some pay on the last day to optimize their cash flow and have personal issues that may require them to hold back funds. Knowing how many of your customers fall into just these two "buckets" would and should be useful information for understanding and targeting customers.

My daughter went to college in Massachusetts and was raised in South Carolina. She needed to go to the emergency room one day to treat an illness and used my health insurance. For seventy-five days I never heard from the hospital about any outstanding bills. When I did receive a bill, it said I owed some money that was not covered by the insurance. Like any good consumer, I called the hospital and asked for a more detailed bill showing what procedures were performed and the cost of those procedures. I viewed this as a valid and necessary request, since the total charg-es were just short of $2,500. Another forty-five days went by and I received the information I requested. I placed the information in my "pay" pile and scheduled it for automatic payment from my checking account. Four days after it was scheduled to be paid, I received a notice from a collection agency indicating I needed to pay the money owed and that the hospital had "extended their services in a prompt and professional manner and we feel certain that you intend to honor this obligation." I called the accounts receivable group at the hospital and asked if they had received my payment. They indicated that they had, but the information was forwarded to the collection agency before that occurred and they would not receive the information about the payment for some time.

I do not expect you to be interested in my daughter's medical condition or by the amount of money involved. This is also not an indictment of the health care system or a social commentary about big business and the individual. It is an excellent example of a flawed process that would cause me to ask some pointed questions about how my business process worked and was executed:

- ✓ I would want to know that the first indication that a client owed me money took over two months to reach that client.
- ✓ I would want to know that the limited data provided the first time required the client to call and ask for additional information.
- ✓ I would want to know that the client intended to pay and had a date for payment set.
- ✓ I would want to prevent any costs or payments to an outside collection agency when I could possibly use my own resources.

If the hospital had a robust customer relationship management (CRM) process in place,[11] or viewed me as someone who could provide a better understanding of why and how I would pay the money owed, a simple phone call could have achieved

---

11   "Customer relationship management (CRM) is a widely implemented model for managing a company's interactions with customers, clients, and sales prospects." Wikipedia, "Customer relationship management," http://en.wikipedia.org/wiki/CRM_software

all the objectives listed above. The information from that phone call could have, at minimum, been typed into a comment field of the accounts receivable record and later viewed for insight. At the extreme other end of the spectrum, the data could have been entered into a CRM system and a specific script followed to collect the data that would feed analysis.

Technology, as it relates to the operation of business, is not a "black box" that is simply purchased and provides you the value you think you want or expect from spending money on technology. How you choose to implement and execute technology determines how and if it will serve your organization in a creative and progressive manner or as a hammer that you pull out, use, and put away until next required.

I do want to take this moment to state that I am not some idealist who expects the world to run like a well-built Swiss watch (yes, there are still nondigital timepieces). I do know that there are people who do not pay their bills and require some form of incentive to pay. Yes, companies and organizations cannot all afford to pay people to call every customer who is in arrears. They can decide that there are incremental steps and strategic actions to take that would lead to some version of the process just outlined. I provide examples to help clarify my point of view and look to examples in my life and those that I have worked with over the years. If replacing *daughter* with *wife, husband, son,* or *dog* works, then do it. You can replace *hospital* with *store, mechanic, distributor,* or *utility,* if that brings the concept closer to a personal experience that captures the concept. I insert this text to note that there are other reasons and views about how to phrase and articulate examples. I believe in my perspective and can, on occasion, get on my version of a soapbox, but I view the concepts as universal in nature.

Chapter Two

Management and Strategy

————— ※※※※※※※※※※※ —————

Management's role in the acquisition and utilization of technology is critical and long lasting in any organization, yet it is frequently viewed as a cost center and a commodity function that all organizations require. Those who have seen the rise of Google, Amazon, and other web-based enterprises may think of these as search engines or purchase sites used by individuals for a specific purpose. I view them as concepts that have leveraged technology and defined new operating models that need to be understood in terms of your organization and your business processes. I use the term *model* not because of the business models that Google or Amazon have developed but the fundamental concepts they must live by to survive. Let us take just one concept that is fundamental to both Google and Amazon—the amount of time it takes for an action to complete after you type something into your computer screen.

Response time is vital to both Google and Amazon. If someone waits for more than four or five seconds—often less—for something meaningful to happen, they may just look somewhere else for an answer. Clearly, the response time you experience is based on more than just company resources. The speed of your Internet connection, the speed of your computer, how well you maintain your computer system, and various other factors impact speed. Response time is critical to these organizations; it is why cable companies and wireless phone providers are constantly finding ways to improve and charge you for quick response time. I accept this as a fact, and that is why it is puzzling that many organizations have slow computer systems, networks, and Internet communication. It is ironic that when I call a manufacturer of computers to purchase a computer system I hear, "Please wait while my system obtains the information." I am talking about waits of fifteen or twenty seconds until we can move to the next question or topic. This presents me with a quandary: Am I going to buy a computer that I expect to be very fast from the company that does not have fast response time for people buying its products? You may be able to recall an encounter within your own company, your wireless provider, a retail chain, or other service provider where this has occurred. The cartoon character Dilbert has used this material profitably for years.[12] This contradiction is obvious to me, but not, apparently, to the company on the other end of the phone.

Management is the group that establishes how and when resources, both financial and human, are used to meet strategic objectives. I do not know if management of the computer company knows that people wait long periods of time, once they reach a living person, because the computer system they use is slow. I am certain that management monitors how long it takes a customer to reach a living person and how long the customer and agent stay on the phone talking, but I do not know if it monitors the speed of network and computer screens used by its employees or outsourced

12   "Dilbert is an American comic strip written and drawn by Scott Adams. First published on April 16, 1989, Dilbert is known for its satirical office humor about a white-collar, micromanaged office featuring the engineer Dilbert as the title character." Wikipedia, "Dilbert," http://en.wikipedia.org/wiki/Dilbert

call center. Irony is not something I would want a customer to think about during a business transaction. The question of computer response time may have been a topic during budgeting discussions, and perhaps it lost funding to new product development (NPD) or marketing, but how can this topic be so far down in the chain of priorities or not be a topic of discussion at all? Google and Amazon have set an expectation for consumers about response time and the speed, quality, and value of information that should be expected from a company. This expectation is not only for consumers but also for the employees of these companies. This is where the strategy aspect becomes relevant and the view of information technology (IT) as an asset or cost center is most relevant. Upgrading networks, computer centers, laptops, and desktops is decidedly a cost, and the associated depreciation reduces the income reported to investors if you are in a publically owned company.[13] I argue that this investment is directly linked to the ability of the company to be profitable and for the employees to feel valued.

Information technology is a cost for the organization, but so is the salary of its chief executive officer. Organizations look to groups like Gartner Research to understand what the standard industry cost of IT is relative to companies their size and in their lines of business.[14] This is important information to know and reference, but the strategic question is, what role do you want IT to have in your organization, and how will it support the goal of achieving success? The answer to this question should drive the cost of your organization's IT structure and not existing business models that execute IT activities with a common infrastructure and methodologies. Information technology touches 98 percent of everyone who works and interacts with an organization. To view IT as a cost or commodity for your organization is equiva-

---

13   "Depreciation refers to two very different but related concepts: The decrease in value of assets (fair value depreciation), and the allocation of the cost of assets to periods in which the assets are used (depreciation with the matching principle)." Wikipedia, "Depreciation", http://en.wikipedia.org/wiki/Depreciation

14   "Gartner is an information technology research and advisory company providing technology related insight." Wikipedia, "Gartner," http://en.wikipedia.org/wiki/Gartner

lent to saying that your NPD costs are necessary but not strategic. Optimizing the effectiveness of your employees is tied to the optimization of your internal technology and your employees' ability to leverage and optimize the technology required while executing their responsibilities.

This brings us full circle. There is an expectation set by the successful industry leaders about the response time expected. This can be achieved with management's strategic plan, which places value and importance on the basic premise of response time. Employees are provided the infrastructure and informed of the purpose and value of rapid response time and this enables great customer service when optimized and executed correctly. This is a philosophy about the value of response time and the role it should play both within and outside the organization. If the cost of taking one second off response time is $100 million dollars, weigh it against the cost of, for example, spending less on an advertising campaign. It may be determined that it is not a viable option, but the important point is that this topic was evaluated and there was a value placed on it.

Another way to implement the concept of strategic IT is to imbed it in the hiring process. If I were to interview someone for the role of vice president of sales and was given two individuals who both had good résumés, a history of achieving objectives, and adequate knowledge about the market my organization served, I would give greater weight to the individual who asked certain types of questions:

How does your organization measure the characteristics of sales? This tells me that there is an understanding about what and how sales metrics are analyzed, and whether repeat sales occur, upselling occurs,[15] different classes of

---

15   "Upselling (sometimes 'up-selling') is a sales technique whereby a seller induces the customer to purchase more expensive items, upgrades, or other add-ons in an attempt to make a more profitable sale." Wikipedia, "Upselling," http://en.wikipedia.org/wiki/Upselling

customers have been established, there are loss leaders,[16] and whether other tactical measures are in place that the organization may track.

What tools does your sales team utilize to identify possible opportunities and close sales? A good indication that there is an expectation of customer targeting based on market analysis and a strategy that targets specific market segments.[17]

If one candidate asked these types of questions and the other did not, I would most likely hire the candidate who had asked them. Having someone who can sell and who also understands why and how sales are measured is valuable, and it is likely to encourage other sales employees to work toward some of these same goals. There is a lot of technology behind the answers to these questions, and a strategy that enables these tools and data to be available.

Information technology has a role in all organizations and management determines how it is positioned and presented to the organization. Having a seat at the highest level of management is vital. In the past, IT was often placed under the chief financial officer (CFO) because accounting and finance is where IT first entered most organizations. This is no longer an appropriate position for IT, and that is why organizations have created the chief information officer (CIO[18]) role and why the CIO sits at the same table as the CFO. Information technology cannot correctly

---

16   "A loss leader, or simply a leader, is a product sold at a low price (at cost or below cost) to stimulate other profitable sales." Wikipedia, "Loss leader," http://en.wikipedia.org/wiki/Loss_leader

17   " A group of people that share one or more characteristics. Each market segment is unique and marketing managers decide on various criteria to create their target market(s). They may approach each segment differently, after fully understanding the needs, lifestyles, demographics and personality of the target." Investopedia "Definition of ' Market Segment'," http://www.investopedia.com/terms/m/market-segment.asp

18   "Chief Information Officer (CIO) or Information Technology (IT) Director is a job title commonly given to the most senior executive in an enterprise responsible for the information technology and computer systems that support enterprise goals. Information technology and its systems have become so important that the CIO has come to be viewed in many organizations as the key contributor in formulating strategic goals for an organization." Wikipedia, "Chief Information Officer," http://en.wikipedia.org/wiki/Chief_information_officer.

serve an organization without being where strategy and funding are fundamentally determined; it stratifies the organization. The needs of human resources, marketing, NPD, customer service, and finance all need to be balanced in a manner that best supports the strategic objectives of the organization. This position also allows management to be informed of the possibilities that exist for IT to assist in meeting the goals and objectives discussed. Reading an article about how Steve Jobs transformed personnel communication and human interfaces does not convey the knowledge required to understand the options IT offers.[19] This is not a mere example, but something that truly happens in the real world. The vice presidents of marketing, finance, and engineering exist because their disciplines require a unique set of knowledge and experience. This is also true of IT; it needs to be at the table for strategy determination. Otherwise, IT will react to strategy instead of influencing it (see fig. 2.1).

19   "The user interface, in the industrial design field of human-machine interaction, is the space where interaction between humans and machines occurs." Wikipedia, "User interface," http://en.wikipedia.org/wiki/User_interface

Figure 2.1. Organizational Structures

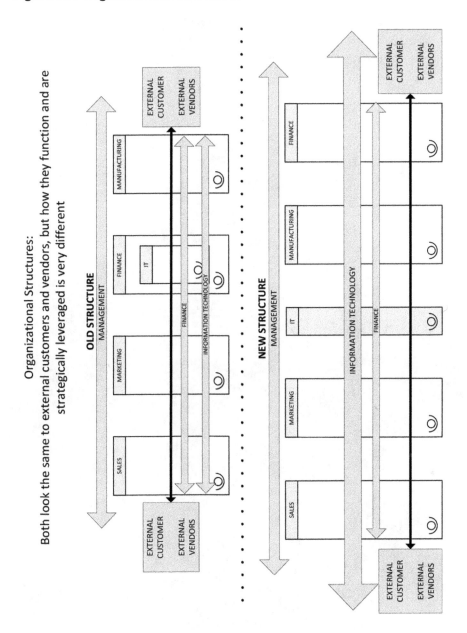

Organizational Structures:
Both look the same to external customers and vendors, but how they function and are strategically leveraged is very different

Chapter Three

Make Information Technology Work for You Rather Than You Work for Information Technology

——————— ⪼⪼⪼⪼⪼⪼⪼⪼⪼⪼⪼ ———————

There are remarkably few key moving parts that need to be fully vetted to generate the correct results from any technology implementation. The "black box" of technology is not magic and does not require a huge language of acronyms imbedded in presentations that always have return on investment story lines. A starting point to reference is the baggage-handling system at Denver International Airport. The amount of publicity generated by this failed implementation and the lessons are well outlined in the following abstract from Ramiro Montealegre's "What Can We Learn from the Implementation of the Automated Baggage-Handling System at the Denver International Airport?"[20]

Over time as changes in the context and in various internal components of the DIA project took place, and the technology began to experience problems related to its newness, management was caught without the tools, time, or structures to facilitate the required changes in operational processes. As the pressure grew, different views began to appear which resulted in open conflict. The process of interaction between the management team, the system development contractor, and the airlines involved a clash of perspectives. There is no evidence, however, that management sought clarification or that it fully understood the magnitude of the problem until the opening of the new airport had to be postponed. After delaying the opening of the new airport three times, the plans for the systems were scaled down from an airport-wide system to a single baggage-handling system for each concourse. During this stage, however, the system implementation management team (now consisting of United Airlines, an airport technology consultant firm, and BAE) facilitated desired changes in this area by sensitive management of the process of change, such as encouraging the extensive dialogue needed between interested parties. Appropriate efforts were made at the various managerial levels involved to avoid problems of coordination. The implementation of the IT system was consciously monitored allowing management to refresh and adapt the strategy for change over time. Six months after the de-scaling of the system, the airport was able to open and operate successfully.

---

20   Ramiro Montealegre, "What Can We Learn from the Implementation of the Automated Baggage-Handling System at the Denver International Airport?" Paper presented at the Association for Information Systems 1996 Americas Conference

Another example of a failed implementation would be the US Air Force installing a new software system, as noted in this excerpt from a *New York Times* article by Randall Stross:

> For the United States Air Force, installing a new software system has certainly proved to be a wicked problem. Last month, it canceled a six-year-old modernization effort that had eaten up more than $1 billion. When the Air Force realized that it would cost another $1 billion just to achieve one-quarter of the capabilities originally planned—and that even then the system would not be fully ready before 2020—it decided to decamp.
>
> Silicon Valley sees its share of software projects that end unhappily. The most expensive failures, however, involve acquisitions of entire companies with software assets that turn out to be far less valuable than thought. Those can lead to stunning write-downs in the billions, as Hewlett-Packard has been forced to take recently.
>
> But the Air Force's software was not some mystery package, nor was it written from scratch. It was commercial off-the-shelf software, or "COTS" (the military can't seem to resist any chance to use an acronym).
>
> Installing COTS to run an enterprise is not a straightforward matter. The Air Force would have to make myriad adjustments to accommodate its individual needs, and in a military setting that would mean meetings and more meetings, unlike anything ever experienced in a Silicon Valley company. Still, it is hard to understand how the Defense Department blew a billion dollars before the plug was pulled.
>
> The software initiative, called the Expeditionary Combat Support System, was supposed to manage logistics using

software from Oracle. In 2006, the Air Force announced that it had awarded a $628 million contract to the Computer Sciences Corporation to serve as lead system integrator; its job would be to "configure, deploy and conduct training and change management activities" before the launch.

Four years later, in 2010, the Air Force said it had pilot programs under way at two bases. In remarks made at the time by Grover Dunn, the Air Force director of transformation, we can see just how unrealistic the project was: "We've never tried to change all the processes, tools and languages of all 250,000 people in our business at once, and that's essentially what we're about to do."[21]

The steps that follow are straightforward, and do not require knowledge about the speed of central processing units.[22] These steps are the tools of a philosophy about how to break down a process that utilizes technology, and will prevent the outcomes just presented.

Step 1. Define success.
Step 2. Start simple and build in the complexity; do not start with complexity and later simplify.
Step 3. Avoid acronyms.
Step 4. Make no assumptions.
Step 5. Determine where the business rules of your organization will reside and be enforced.
Step 6. Employ visualization.
Step 7. Create a prototype very early in the process.

---

21 Randall Stross, "Billion-Dollar Flop: Air Force Stumbles on Software Plan," New York Times, December 9, 2012.

22 " A central processing unit (CPU), also referred to as a central processor unit, is the hardware within a computer that carries out the instructions of a computer program by performing the basic arithmetical, logical, and input/output operations of the system." Wikipedia, "Central processing unit," http://en.wikipedia.org/wiki/CPU

Step 8. Control the data entered at the point of entry.

Step 9. Educate all individuals about their roles in the processes and their contributions to the overall organization.

Step 1. Define Success

A fundamentally straightforward and logical objective is to define success. I would suggest that the definition of success is the effective completion of a task executed within the parameters of time and money outlined. Defining success may be the realization of the results: decreased customer turnover, increased upselling to existing customers, and a better understanding of your customers' needs. Whatever the definition ultimately is, it is critical that it is fully internalized by the group implementing and executing the task. Keeping the definition of success at the forefront prevents the multitude of activities, decisions, and challenges from diluting the purity of the definition. As basic as this statement sounds, the mutation of the original definition of success is often an option, and the pressures from time and money to make incremental changes can cause the final result to be very different from that originally intended.

Rationalization of why and how changes are made is much easier than many would think possible. It is unrealistic to believe that changes will not be made and compromises reached, but it is not unrealistic to expect them not to alter direction and intent so much that the definition of success must be changed. The hardest part of this process is coming to grips with indications that timelines, capabilities, and money estimates were incorrect and need to be reassessed. If visualization and prototypes have been completed, there is a good possibility that the gaps are not large and adjustments are not substantial in nature. If the situation is similar to the baggage-handling system at the Denver International Airport, your definition of success or your methods of achieving success may change. Whatever the outcome, the definition of success should be the directional force determining next steps.

Step 2. Start Simple and Build in the Complexity; Do Not Start with Complexity and Later Simplify

If your local information technology (IT) team or consultants are implementing and building the systems, the most important part of the process is the design. There may be three or three hundred moving parts to the system and process, but you need to understand the concepts and the logic. Albert Einstein once said, "If you can't explain it simply, you don't understand it well enough." The concepts and technology utilized cannot and should not prevent this rule from being executed. You can be building a particle accelerator or a baggage-handling system, but the individuals involved should be able to explain the concepts, risks, and functionality in terms that others can understand and internalize. The absence of this basic requirement tells you a great deal and is the first red flag that you should recognize. There are a few standard "push backs" that are always encountered when someone outside of the implementation process challenges concepts or methodologies presented:

- *You are not familiar with the technology and concepts. We will take this off-line and review it with you individually.* This dismissive technique is a classic attempt to make you look and feel less knowledgeable about the topic.
- *You are resistant to change and are not embracing the new technology and processes.* The intent of this technique is to place you in the "other camp" and prevent others from joining in your line of questioning.
- *We are reviewing high level concepts, and not the details of implementation and functionality.* This statement is appropriate only during the vendor/technology evaluation process. During this process, there is limited time and the key points of interest need to be covered. Once the process starts, this answer is no longer appropriate.

There are times when someone really just does not understand the train of thought or process presented. It is then the responsibility of the team to indicate that the conversation should continue at a different time and place. A good meeting moderator will confirm that all others have a clear understanding and that the follow-up conversation actually takes place.

Starting simple does not mean that only simple steps should be executed. *Simple* means the fundamental aspects of the process and technology are presented and understood by the consumers. If multiple options exist at different points, the reason that one is chosen over another should be provided.

Step 3. Avoid Acronyms

Unless you are presenting gravitational theories to a group of astrophysicists who have all worked with you for years and read your presentation before hearing you speak, acronyms are the best way to introduce misunderstanding and errant dialogue. I am often not sure what advantage undefined acronyms offer, except for the obvious reduction in words. When acronyms are presented, their meaning and relevance should be clearly stated. Your audience may change over time, or you may want to reuse pieces of your presentation, and acronyms will gain you very little, if anything. I have come to interpret acronyms as a way of speaking to a smaller audience within your discipline or organization and excluding your conversation from a larger audience.

Step 4. Make No Assumptions

The saying "Never assume, you'll just make and ass out of you and me" may be an understatement. Visualization, prototypes, and the avoidance of acronyms are important because words are understood in the context of the recipient's knowledge and experiences. I have been in many meetings in which everyone hears the same words and then walks away with very different understandings and thoughts about the subject discussed. It is the presenter's responsibility to avoid as many assumptions as possible and for the recipients to ask questions about areas not fully understood. Any meeting that has individuals multitasking will garner incorrect assumptions as a result. The process of integrating IT into business processes is riddled with opportunities for incorrect assumptions and misunderstandings. Assumptions are also the result of overgeneralized presentations that do not expose the "weeds" of the topic presented. In a time of increasing integration, evolution, and demise of entire business models, it is difficult to believe that simplification of the presentation process would not lead to incorrect assumptions. If you add the desire for innovation and creativity, the possibility multiplies. I am willing to bet a dinner that there were some very fundamental assumptions, unintentionally made, about the baggage-handling system at the Denver International Airport.

Step 5. Determine Where the Business Rules of Your Organization Will Reside and Be Enforced

Business rules may be strategic in nature (i.e., differentiating your business from others), may be rules of payment (i.e., the client must pay before shipment takes place), may involve the configuration of the item being purchased (i.e., it must be blue and open from the top), or might dictate any number of parameters. The rules decided upon will determine where time and effort will be invested. Rule enforcement can be done in a transparent manner or in a hidden manner. Transparency means having tables that contain the rules and can be reviewed and maintained through human interfaces. Hidden rules involve having some form of code written that one must wade through in order to understand what is to be expected.

Determining business rules is critical to how you will grow and respond to change over time. It is a strategic decision, and not one that should be excluded from the more traditional view of organizational strategy. It is, in fact, the method of assuring that an organizational strategy will be successful. Some view business rules as being too far into the "weeds" of the organization and that management needs to focus on the "big picture." But organizations of the future will win and lose based on what is executed in the "weeds" of highly integrated organizational processes. Business rules need to be tightly linked to strategy and often, but not always, need to be shaped and implemented based on a macrostrategy. Business rules, at a macrolevel, cover how organizational groups follow business practices and how they bind together the processes; they determine how well the organization will function. These include the rules associated with budgets and the rules of interaction between organizational groups. If management stays out of the "weeds," it will endure the consequences of having them grow.

I will present an example of this concept and carry it through some of the standard activities of any organization.

One of the strategic goals of an organization is to be customer-intimate. This is currently a popular objective, one that can be defined and implemented in many ways. For this example, I will define one aspect of intimacy as ensuring that customer information is correct and up to date at all times because your product depends on the existence of accurate contact information. To execute this strategy, you review all the points of contact your customers have with your organization. You identify that your call center is the most likely first encounter point and your website is the next most likely point of contact. These are followed by your sales organization and then by your service organization. I will present one of many possible scenarios of how fundamental processes are developed and altered in an organization.

Your company has evolved over time and you have a Call Center with software designed to support its activities. This software has a master customer table that links to phone numbers of your customers, and when someone calls, the name, address, and contact information is captured. You have an accounting system that bills these customers, and it only requires a billing address and full name for each customer. The call center may have this address, a separate shipping address, and a business address that

was used once by this customer. The accounts receivable group
has an address it required to open the account, but it does not
receive notices of any change of address.

The company grows, purchasing an ERP system to handle its
financial and manufacturing systems, and this replaces the current accounts receivable system but not the call center software
because the ERP system is not designed to handle customer calls.
The ERP system obtains its address information from the old accounts receivable system, along with that system's inability to
update address changes. The ERP system also receives some—
but not all—of the addresses from the call center system because
it does not have structures to support all the addresses stored in
the call center software. Over the years of growth and changes
at the company, the people who understood how and why the
call center and accounts receivable systems were separate (and
required updating when the billing address changed) have been
replaced by new people who know the ERP software but have
limited understanding of the software, processes, and people
working in the call center.

The accounts receivable group starts to notice that the number of bad addresses on bills is increasing, and there is a meeting that determines there is poor communication between the
call center and the accounts receivable group regarding address
changes. After a review, it is noted that the amount of time and
effort required to automate the process of changes in the call center to the ERP accounts receivable system would take four times
longer and cost five times as much as establishing a manual process. In addition, the company website has been linked to the
customer relationship management (CRM) system—which the
sales department purchased to support its understanding of customer touchpoints[23]—but not to the ERP system. Activities of the

---

23   Touchpoint (also touch point, contact point, customer contact, point of contact, brand touchpoint,
      and customer touchpoint) is the interface of a product, a service or a brand with customers, non-
      customers, employees and other stakeholders—before, during and after a transaction, respec-
      tively. This applies for business-to-business as well as business-to-consumer markets." Wikipedia,
      "Touchpoint," http://en.wikipedia.org/wiki/Touchpoint

service organization are merged into the ERP system, and some information goes to the CRM system from a weekly batch process that runs on weekends to minimize impact on other processes run in the ERP system. Finally, the IT group was brought in to outline how best to keep these various systems functioning, in a cost-effective but rapid manner.

I am stopping this narrative at this point not because I could not continue or because I lack additional material about this process but because each functional group in the organization was executing its job based on its objectives and within its budget, and there was a linkage to the overall organizational objective of achieving customer intimacy. The decisions made were directionally correct and explainable given the resources and time allotted.

Now, let's step back and examine the overall strategic goal of achieving customer intimacy. There are two critical points about the scenario outlined. First, customers do not know about the systems, groups, budgets, or processes of your organization, nor do they care about them. They want to know that if they provide information to any touchpoint in your organization it is reflected the next time data are required. Second, customer intimacy is not something that can be implemented independently by various functional groups through various functional systems. It is a macrostrategy that needs to be funded and orchestrated by those groups and individuals that are part of the process. It is not a cost that is to be carried by the sales, service, or IT departments but by the company. In many ways, the actions just outlined are "death by a thousand cuts." Functional groups attempting to achieve a corporate objective without centralized leadership and funding to bind them cohesively together will incur this fate. When confronted with the information about the time and cost of automating the data feed from the call center to the ERP system it is a decision for the company, not the call center or of the ERP group. Does the time and effort required bring the company closer to a strategic objective? Is it being done in a manner that limits the amount of nonvalue-added activities? Does it effectively and efficiently support the company going forward? Does it lay a foundation that will not have to be replaced in the near future?

Customer intimacy is an excellent strategic objective, and it is easier to talk about than to execute fully within an organization. The true cost and effort to execute this strategy is often hidden from management by views that are incremental and not holistic. This brings me back to the implementation of business rules. The business rules enforced by the company and through software — at all levels of operation — need to support the strategic objectives in a macromanner and not a micromanner. It is vital to recognize that business rules are imbedded in processes and software, much like the veins found in marble stone. If the visualization of this strategy is executed in a holistic manner, the threads of the process outlined above would be obvious and the nature and cost of the strategy accurately presented.

Step 6. Employ Visualization

Visualization takes the concepts expressed in step 1 and gives them a physical presence so everyone concerned can review them. It is used by publications like the *New York Times* to convey multiple concepts and facts in a way that removes the challenges of using only words to convey an idea or concept. I have seen visualization used to explain financial and political concepts very effectively. The art of visualization is explained in the books of Edward R. Tufte,[24] which should be read by anyone interested in this concept.

Visualization includes an aspect that could potentially be a separate step: it needs to include some basic conceptualization of what the output of the process of change will be. With what end result in mind is change taking place? The visualization may

---

24   "Tufte's writing is important in such fields as information design and visual literacy, which deal with the visual communication of information. He coined the term "chartjunk" to refer to useless, noninformative, or information-obscuring elements of quantitative information displays." Wikipedia, "Edward Tufte," http://en.wikipedia.org/wiki/Edward_Tufte

encapsulate the change, but often there are specific reports or structures that are expected from the implementation of change. Generating a basic example of what that expected output should be is all part of the process of visualization. It should be a basic step that everyone can agree represents the successful execution of change. It also confirms that change can in fact generate the end results desired. It is hard to overvalue the aspect of visualization. People think they understand, think they know something can be done, and think everyone has the same vision. Group visualization will confirm or deny these thoughts, and will prevent some very painful and seemingly impossible negative results.

Figure 3.1 represents how time, meetings, improved customer satisfaction, and improvements in costs and margin could be presented for a fictitious project. Ultimately, when asked a question about a specific step or process in your project, you should be able to point to a specific visual aid and add some basic context for the individual asking the question. This process does take time, but it is a vastly less expensive and less complicated method of developing a repeatable, visual, and explainable outline of a project and the processes involved.

Figure 3.1. Visualization: fictitious project to improve cost, margins, customer satisfaction and cash flow.

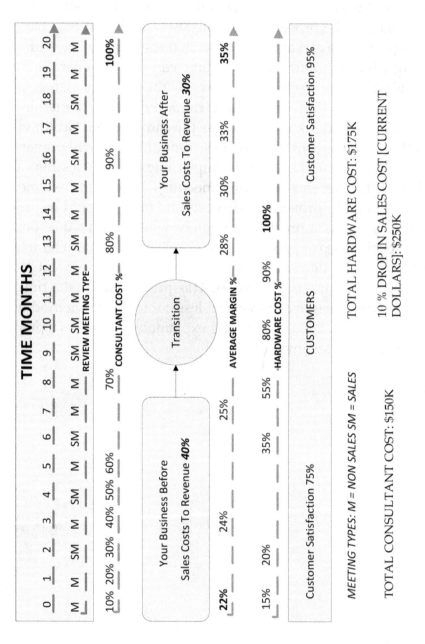

In my opinion, robust visualizations are not prepared and presented frequently for several reasons. First, they are harder to execute. Presenting several bullet points and talking to those points is faster and does not require the clarity, crispness, or risk that a well-thought-out image requires. But the phrase "A picture is worth a thousand words" has great merit. The stark ability of an image to highlight the strengths and weakness of the concept presented is always underestimated. There is a real possibility that the creation of such an image will be the last step of a process because of the clarity it can bring to a discussion. With visualization there is less time spent explaining the bullet points and more time explaining the nuances of the topic.

Second, PowerPoint presentations are often distilled down to very basic and fundamental concepts for management consumption. I no longer believe in this process or reasoning. The concepts and details, which are intentionally reduced to only a few high level bullet points, can obscure the complexities and scope of decisions which need to be made for one concept but has derivative impacts. As I outlined earlier, the pervasive impact of information technology makes narrowed-down views of impact and scope less strategic than they would be if placed in a broader setting. Visualization allows the current topic and larger issues to be presented at the same time, and for the conversation to be about the specific issue within the broader topic. (As an analogy, blinders are placed on racehorses specifically to keep them from being influenced by the other horses and activity around them.) I realize that distilled-down Microsoft PowerPoint presentations are intended to make for "crisp" dialogue and lead to decisions, but in the highly integrated and interdependent environments of modern business they can lead to decisions that resolve smaller-scale issues but do not address them in a more holistic and strategic manner.

Third, it takes longer to visualize than it does to generate bullet points. Visualization may require a larger set of skills or require additional assistance. A good PowerPoint presentation can be converted into a visual model, or a visual model can be added.

Step 7. Create a Prototype Very Early in the Process

Nothing is better than seeing and understanding what will or will not happen. Do not let anyone tell you that you cannot create a prototype or see an existing example of how tasks will be done. Prototyping is often thought to be an unnecessary or more costly approach to implementation and is often avoided or dropped for these reasons. Like visualization, prototyping is one of the most visual methods of examining the nature and impact of new processes and tools. Architects have used prototypes to explain and present their vision and concepts so that others can internalize them. Again, I am not naive enough to think that an entire ERP system can be simulated, but existing systems can be watched, reviewed, and challenged, taking into account the needs and concepts of your organization. Unless you are breaking entirely new ground in your area of business, there are existing models that consultants or associations can allow you to interact with on some level of detail. If you are breaking entirely new ground, a prototype may be required, but here the first step would be to create something more like a movie storyboard. A prototype based on the storyboard may then follow.

Step 8. Control the Data Entered at the Point of Entry

Good data are the best tools that IT can provide to an organization. The adage "You only get to make a first impression once" is also true about accurate data. At the very bottom of every IT integrated business process are data about something. This may be another painfully obvious statement that evokes the expression "Duh." The expression "Garbage in, garbage out" exists because it seems painfully obvious.[25] I could call this section the microbusiness rule section and link it to step 5. I am going to outline a very short list of data-entry business rules; if executed

---

25   "Garbage in, garbage out (GIGO) in the field of computer science or information and communications technology refers to the fact that computers will unquestioningly process the most nonsensical of input data, 'garbage in', and produce nonsensical output, 'garbage out'.... It is also commonly used to describe failures in human decision-making due to faulty, incomplete, or imprecise data." Wikipedia, "Garbage in, Garbage Out," http://en.wikipedia.org/wiki/Garbage_in,_garbage_out.

consistently and without variation, they will assure that large numbers of people will not have to spend their time attempting to interpret, correct, or rearrange the data previously entered. In addition, you will have a system and process that users can better control and adapt to changes in business processes and customer demands.

- Data entered will not have leading or trailing spaces or numerous spaces in between characters. There is a basic function in most IT tools, "trim," that performs this process. Unless you have experienced the pain of not enforcing this rule, it may be hard to conceptualize. The most basic example I can provide is "1" versus " 1". The space in front of the second number 1 not only looks bad but means that this is not a numeric field; it is an alphanumeric field that allows most characters to be entered.

- If you expect a number, make sure the field is numeric. If you expect an alphanumeric field, make sure the user knows this. The amount of pain and suffering that this will avoid to manipulators, consumers, and presenters of data is beyond explanation. The true value of this rule is based in the technical manner in which databases and query tools interpret numbers and alphanumeric characters. The philosophy that numbers should be numbers and alphanumerics should be alphanumerics can and will cost time and money. Making it a clear requirement will smooth out the impact and cost. Finally, dates are stored in a different manner, so if it is a date make sure it is a date.

- If data should be one or more values from an existing table structure, make the data come from that table structure. Another way of expressing this point is the creation of a "pick list." This functionality exists in large ERP systems and in Microsoft Excel. If you want a field to be entered as blue, red or green, then create a location where those three values exist and link it to the entry point where those values need to exist. When someone comes to this data entry point, they can only select one of the three colors. You can also add attributes to the colors. You can have the number 1 associated with blue, the number 2 associated with red, and the number 3 associated with green. Having the values you expect or require confirmed by an external data table establishes a structure of control as well as expected results that will forever benefit the consumers of the data. If an effective date is added to each of these data elements in the table, you can have them be valid for entry for a period of time and then not available for use at some future date. (Chapter 11 has a more detailed explanation.) The ultimate value of this structure is that users can maintain the contents of these tables and control the quality and nature of large amounts of data without IT involvement. This approach will require more time to develop systems and processes, but the number of nonvalue activities that will be avoided downstream will be significant and meaningful.

These are three rules a non-IT person can request from whatever integrated system is being developed or conceptualized. I have developed systems that imposed these rules, and the changes made over the years were not to correct data or resolve issues created by bad data but were instead in the interests of adding functionality. This is the best definition of success: spending time and resources to add functionality to processes and not adding people and controls to manage the lack of accurate data downstream in the organization.

Step 9. Educate All Individuals about Their Roles in the Processes and Their Contributions to the Overall Organization
Education is the final step of any good IT process implementation, and providing insight as to how and why it is important to the user/implementer is the final step that needs to be taken.

My earlier reference to the saying "There are no small parts, only small actors" is especially true in the world of IT. One of the great benefits of developing and implementing well-designed IT systems is that users spend more time doing their job effectively and creatively. Every minute someone does not question the accuracy or validity of the data they are seeing or analyzing is a minute that can be used to further the strategy and purpose of your organization. Every person who has ever been sent an e-mail, letter, report, or software product that does not contain what they expected or that operates in a manner that is not understood can relate to this concept. Being part of the process also means you have a role in the process, even if you did not conceptualize, create, or implement that process and the tools used. Employees in the accounts payable department validating bills from vendors are playing a strategic role in the supply chain management process.[26] The quality of their work may be the result of some great work and thought executed upstream in the organization, but quality of execution is tied, to some degree, by understanding how their actions add value to the process. Creative thoughts and activities are not generated by individuals who feel they are executing a task that is repetitive and of less value than those in the research and development department. In fact, supply chain management depends on accurate and timely data about what vendors provide and cost over time. You will know if the work and effort has generated the benefit and value outlined when the user/implementer sees the value and eventually shows you how the process can be improved.

Education will involve two distinct segments: one for those involved in the actual process of executing the project, and one for those who will utilize the results of the project. Both are important, and each will have unique characteristics. It is important

---

26   "Supply chain management (SCM) is the management of a network of interconnected businesses involved in the ultimate provision of product and service packages required by the end customers in a supply chain." Wikipedia, "Supply Chain Management," http://en.wikipedia.org/wiki/Supply_chain_management.

to remember that the individuals who were involved in the project will have understandings and knowledge gained over time. The consumers of the results generally have only been exposed to concepts and secondhand conversations. Education of the consumer is where the rubber meets the road; it is not where time should be saved or resources reduced. This is the end game, and it needs to be given the time and resources required to succeed. Often, there is a certain amount of project fatigue, and this becomes a victim of management's and participants' being ready to move on to the next thing. Do not let that happen.

Figure 3.2. The Process Outlined as a Methodology

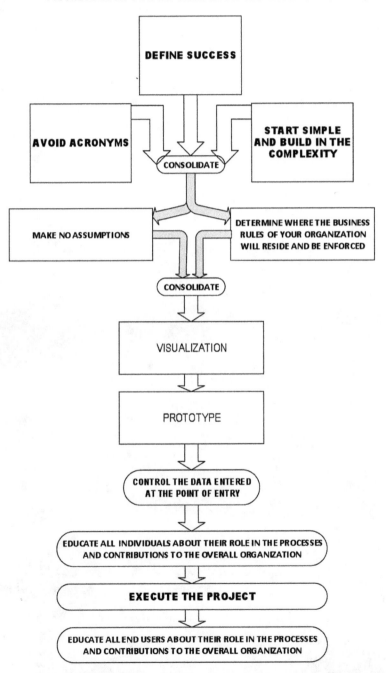

A PHILOSOPHY FOR INFORMATION TECHNOLOGY PROCESS

Chapter Four

People Execute, Perform, React, and Function within the Limits of the Technology They Have Available

Cultural theories concentrate on the experiences, cultural values, attitude, and beliefs that are shared by people within an organization and the effect these have on how people interrelate. In the book *Organizational Culture and Leadership*, cultural theorist Edgar Schein claims that organizational behaviors will be what result from the values your employees have gotten used to applying at the place of business as well as their usual approach to work.[27]

If you give a group of people on a deserted island rope, rocks, buckets and trees, they will find the best way to create a safe place to sleep, the best way to obtain food and water, and the

---

[27]   Edgar Schein, *Organizational Culture and Leadership*, 4th ed. (San Francisco: Jossey-Bass, 2010). For more on organizational behavior theories, go to http://www.organizationalbehaviortheories. net/.

best way to protect themselves using these items. If you give people a laptop, spreadsheet, network, and accounting software and tell them to run a business, they will run the business using the tools provided. They may invent ways to accomplish their objectives or just optimize the tools they have available. The important point is that people will work with what they have available to accomplish the task given to them. Information technology (IT) is a collection of tools that provides a predefined opportunity to execute a set of tasks. It establishes the electronic walls and rooms that people will operate within for some length of time. How intelligently you build the walls and rooms will determine how intelligently people perform within this space.

If I build a house with five rooms that are twelve feet square, three hallways that are ten feet long by four feet wide, and six doors that are six feet tall and four feet wide, then I have defined, by default, several other important items: the size of the furniture I can bring in through the doors and hallways, the total amount of stuff I can bring in, and the patterns of traffic that will take place within the space. My first decisions set the limits and boundaries for my future decisions, and if they are not forward thinking in nature they will limit or cause additional work. Decisions made about IT have a very similar nature, and will impact all individuals within an organization who work with and rely on it.

The decisions made about the hardware, infrastructure, and functionality of your IT will drive behavior as much as your compensation incentives plan. The boundaries and understanding about the infrastructure will establish patterns of behavior that can be favorable or unfavorable over time. There is an element of behavioral science that should be utilized when building the IT infrastructure.[28] What behavior do you want the individuals

---

28   "The term behavioural sciences encompasses all the disciplines that explore the activities of and interactions among organisms in the natural world. It involves the systematic analysis and investigation of human and animal behaviour through controlled and naturalistic observation, and disciplined scientific experimentation. It attempts to accomplish legitimate, objective conclusions through rigorous formulations and observation..... Examples of behavioural sciences include psychology, cognitive science, and anthropology. Wikipedia, "Behavioural Sciences," http://en.wikipedia.org/wiki/Behavioural_sciences.

of my organization to display? If you would like them to be able to walk around, talk with others, and collaborate in an ad-hoc manner, then you should have a high-speed wireless network, and each individual should have a portable IT device that allows or promotes this type of organizational behavior. The impact and limitations that are created by IT infrastructure decisions are not unimportant; they are strategic and can have great impact.

Software has a fixed number of capabilities, and it is designed to execute a set of functions that meet some need of an organization or individual. Creatively using and understanding this functionality is where there is opportunity for innovation and new thinking. One of the most interesting and creative adaptations I have read about was related to football. The concept of looking at the rules and patterns followed by literally everyone, and studying the actual statistics and nature of a standard behavior, made me step back and consider what opportunities exist in the world of IT to do something similar. It is very important to recognize that there are lessons to learn from many different disciplines, and ways to incorporate them into other, apparently unrelated, disciplines.

Kevin Kelley, the head football coach of Pulaski Academy in Little Rock, Arkansas, analyzed what happened when his team punted the football on fourth downs. He determined that the math indicated running a standard play would be a better course of action. His team stopped punting and began running plays on fourth downs. Punting is now the exception for his team, and they win a lot of football games.[29] For Kelley to have challenged such a fundamentally established course of action and endured the criticism that must have followed his decision is inspiring. What I have learned from this is that there may be actions I can take within the boundaries of the IT world that challenge conventional wisdom and doctrine and might improve the daily functions I affect.

---

29   John Wertheim, "Down 29-0 before Touching the Ball," *Sports Illustrated Online*, September 15, 2011, http://sportsillustrated.cnn.com/2011/writers/scorecasting/09/15/kelley.pulaski/index. html; Kevin Fedotin, "Arkansas Coach Punts Traditional Game Plan," http://highschool.rivals. com/content.asp?CID=892888.

A story from a high school friend also triggered some examination and reinforced my belief in thinking differently about what we consider to be normal processes. My friend went to law school and became a bankruptcy lawyer; he developed a relationship with a venture capitalist and he would join him in the process of evaluating opportunities presented for funding. I asked why he was brought in to help in these evaluations and he said, "Because I know what can and does go wrong with companies and individuals, and he wanted that perspective." If innovation is a topic that you would like to read more about, an interesting look at innovation can be found in Jon Gertner's *The Idea Factory: Bell Labs and the Great Age of American Innovation*.[30]

Social media has highlighted a transition in how technology is interpreted. Who would have predicted that social media would be given a prominent role in the Arab Spring and that people would find interest in sending 140 charter strings of text via Twitter? Much is now written about how social media can impact business in a meaningful and effective manner, justifying money being spent and individuals being hired to execute these social media related functions. It is vital that there be a philosophy about how technology is brought into an organization and what role it will play in the strategic plans in place. As always, technology is very, very sexy, but is it useful? To put on your sociological glasses and look at your entire IT organization would be a fascinating exercise for any organization.

30　　John Gertner, *The Idea Factory: Bell Labs and the Great Age of American Innovation* (New York: Penguin, 2013).

Chapter Five

Use All Aspects of Your Tools

———— ⧗⧗⧗⧗⧗⧗⧗⧗⧗⧗⧗⧗⧗ ————

Phone, software, and processes: do not leave "clubs out of your bag" because you failed to learn they exist or have not invested the time to master these tools.

Vendors build software and hardware to perform the tasks required and to provide features that make them competitive. If a vendor is providing a "one-stop solution" or a very specific "functional solution," the number of features that are offered and provided in the base solution will attempt to cover that area in a competitive manner.

As an example, take my purchase of a cordless phone for my home's landline. The key features I looked for when making such a purchase were the quality of sound and battery life. When I went deeper into the product features, considered operating frequencies, because other wireless devices share some frequencies and some increase the range of the devices. I also considered security issues associated with the signal, caller ID, a speakerphone feature, and the ability to use a headset, and also features related to storing phone numbers and redialing, among other things. Of all the features available, however, I only truly cared about battery life, sound quality, having a speakerphone, and the phone's frequency. I do not know how to use most of the other features, and really do not care that my phone is capable of doing other tasks. In addition, I skimmed through the manual to set up the phone, but have never looked at it again.

I use this basic example because it translates well to the world of information technology (IT). The software and hardware purchased for business has many features and functions, but how many are utilized, useful in nature, understood by users, and—more important—understood by management and viewed as a strategic asset?

Software purchased will provide some set of functions and options. Ideally, the business solutions designed would leverage the optimal level of functionality and potential value. Now, think about the software you use for personal or business reasons. Do you know all the potential features and functions of Microsoft's Excel, Word, or PowerPoint? Do you know all the capabilities of your e-mail or instant messaging software? Do you know all the capabilities of your phone or multifeatured printer? The total capabilities of many software packages are often not fully implemented or, often, the knowledge of all the features is lost over time. The basic needs and functions of the organization will always drive the use of the standard features or functionality, but there needs to be a conscious decision to explore and investigate the total range of opportunities offered by the software tool purchased. This may sound like common sense, or a true "Duh!"' moment, but leaving functionality and opportunities "on the table" happens daily. I have always found that end users are the most likely and best suited to optimize the tools they employ on a daily basis, but they have to know what is possible or be able to ask someone whether something can be achieved. It is also true that not every idea or concept can be implemented and that the organizational processes may not allow some actions to take place, but understanding strategically what is possible should be a priority of management and all functional groups. Of course, knowing what your end users think and value should be part of the criteria of purchasing software. Yet, tapping into the creative nature of individuals and turning those thoughts into actions needs to be a conscious set of actions planned, supported, and executed by management. Fortunately, capabilities of software often only require organizational process changes and not software modification. Oddly, I have never known managements to spend time on understanding the boundaries of their software tool sets, but they might take courses of action that may or may not be aligned with the functionality of their software tools. I want to review, in greater depth, some of the statements I have made.

Understanding All the Features and Functions of the Software and Hardware Purchased

Depending on the magnitude of impact and total dollars spent, the amount of time and thought that goes into the purchase of software and hardware will vary. The most important aspect of the process, however, is that it has been determined that something new is required, that you want to achieve the basic objectives of the purchase, and you want to leverage this product in your portfolio of software and hardware. Of course, the topics of total cost of ownership, support, and estimated life span will also be considered, but these are subordinate strategically to the previous three points.

You may have reached the conclusion that something new is required for many reasons. "New" always offers opportunity for improvement, even if it is reducing features and functions for a macrostrategy or cost containment. The new purchase must fit into a macro–IT strategy that is aligned with the strategic goals established for the organization. Depending on what is being purchased, you may require consultant support, vendor implementation support, and user education. Determining who within the organization will learn all the features and functions of the product purchased and how those features and functions will or will not be leveraged by the organization is strategic and necessary. How the knowledge of the features and functions will be spread over the organization, and how the knowledge of the unused features and functions will be preserved for reference when new demands are presented, are key tasks to be established and executed. Organizations are striving to be more competitive, leaner, smarter, and more creative. These goals are achieved, in part, by having a baseline of knowledge in each employee about the purpose of the organization and the tools that organization employs. I am not referring to computer-aided design/computer-aided manufacturing (CAD/CAM) software or network routers. I am referring to those tools in front of 99 percent of the individuals of the organization — tools for order management, e-mail, spreadsheets, word processing, and smartphones. Having a sales representative who understands and uses the full features of Microsoft Excel graphing, summarization, and analysis is a true asset. Sales representatives are fed a great deal of data from corporate systems, but my experience has been that successful and versatile individuals take these data and turn them into something specific to the needs of their customers and their view of the business. Ideally, these creative mutations of organizational data have a method of being passed to management and, if found valuable at a macrolevel, turned into the very information sent to sales representatives. If the value is very specific to the customer, the ability for the sales representative to understand that he or she can provide the information, that it makes a difference to the customer, and that is a valuable use of the representative's finite amount of time may be what differentiates one business from another. If cost, features, and functions of your product are basically on par with your competitors, the ability of your sales representative to use the standard tool set more effectively than your competitors do is a competitive asset. In appendix 1, I outline the concept of controlled customization, which allows standardization but includes the ability to adapt standards to the specific needs of your customer without losing the benefits of the standards established.

I am not implying that the same approach and needs do not apply to noncommodity software and hardware products like CAD/CAM software. These are tools for subsets of users in an organization. The same rules of leveraging features and functions apply, and perhaps in a more important manner. A lot of organizations have this type of software, but how do you make it a strategically and functionally superior asset for your organization? There are often one or two individuals who learn the software in great detail and then become the "experts" that act as the support for everyone else using the software. (Google has become an amazing unpaid support group in many IT organizations!) The ability to tap into others for assistance with problems is extremely beneficial, but it is less useful for achieving best practices and finding the best methods to achieve a specific task that does not fall into "standard" task actions.

A final note on this topic. Having worked on various projects, I have come to the conclusion that I would rather have someone who is an expert with Microsoft Excel than someone who is less proficient with Microsoft Access. I would rather have someone who is an expert with Microsoft Access than someone who is less proficient with SQL and relational databases. My logic is very basic. The people who are true experts with a tool find a way to extract answers from the data. Learning software and being creative with software are two different skills. Creativity comes from understanding the needs of the consumers of your work and bending the tool so that it can be the best current and future answer to their needs. People with partial knowledge of tools can execute basic requirements, but they often cannot find ways to answer the more complex and subtle questions that invariably present themselves, or to offer the opportunity to provide a differentiating level of understanding. Highly self-motivated individuals may drive themselves to this level of ability, but to have a broad base of these skill levels requires institutionalization of the training and rewards associated with these abilities. Customer relationship management systems and iPads are great tools, but they can be the equivalent of either a dull or sharp saw to a carpenter. Salespeople will sell their software and hardware based on their features, functions, and possible uses, but using these products to their optimum potential is your responsibility.

End Users Are the Most Likely and Best Suited to Optimizing the Tools They Use on a Daily Basis, but They Have to Know What Is Possible

Having written and modified various software systems, I am constantly amazed at how end users find ways to make software do things they need in ways that I would never have considered. The bottom line is that no matter how much design work I did, end users would internalize the tool and then bend or ask it to be bent to their ever-evolving needs. If I had done my job of creating a foundation that contained the features and functions requested, and understood that mutations would take place, the ever-evolving needs could then be achieved without substantial time and cost. Meeting the immediate requirements requested can be done well or done badly. This is true of every profession I have ever encountered, and IT is no exception to the rule. End users will provide the answer to

1. what they want and do not have
2. what they wish they had

This may not, however, always align with what they will *need*. That is the job of management, but it is a hard topic to correctly identify.

I quickly learned that I could address points 1 and 2 above but had to leave open enough "bolt-on" opportunities to meet the unknown needs. Enterprise resource planning (ERP) systems basically leave a lot of empty data fields that can be defined by the user and leveraged in "back-end" software systems or in some reporting done within ERP systems themselves. Understanding the future objectives and strategy of the organization allows someone to build in future functionality without spending substantial additional funds or time.

Imagine that the organization wants to organize its vendors into different categories and age the bills associated with these categories but does not have the time or resources to execute this task. When reporting is created for the current set of requirements, there can be some structure built that will allow for this type of reporting in the future. This is not extremely difficult, and does not have to cost additional time or money.

This is the difference between a good consultant and a bad consultant, as well as good and bad software or hardware vendors. Consumers are not stupid; they can see when things could have been done more effectively. I have had software vendors who responded to absolute requests with hard-coding rather than thoughtfulness. We replaced those vendors and their software because they could never truly meet the business needs in a manner that did not feel like we were being played for fools.

It Is Uncommon for Management to Spend Time to Understand the Boundaries of Its Software Tool Sets, but It May Take Courses of Action that are Not Aligned to the Functionality of Its Software Tools

This is a more difficult topic to discuss without challenging established management theory or placing excessive weight on technology. I am not naive about the need to make decisions that do not fit nicely into the current structure and technology of an organization; these things do and must happen. Yet there are many more decisions made and actions taken that can recognize the integrated nature of technology and its role within the organization. It is within this area of tactical execution that I address this topic.

By definition, management does less of the technical execution of tasks and more of the discussion about what is or is not done now or in the future. Ideas and issues are discussed and possible solutions outlined without the specific technical issues associated with these choices yet defined. It is at this point that two critical steps need to be executed: One, how do these ideas and solutions fit into the larger strategy of the organization? Two, what actions need to be taken to make the idea and solution fit into the larger strategy of the organization and its IT? The answers to these questions should drive the manner in which the solution is executed. Often the problem presented to the technical executioner of the task is, we have this need, and we would like it executed quickly and with minimum impact to other tasks concurrently being worked on. When presented with this statement a majority of individuals will focus their response to meet the objectives stated. This approach is what would be expected if you outsourced solutions to a vendor and were operating within the guidelines of your contractual agreement. It is not the approach to take when internal resources are used to fulfill the task, however. Internal resources should be given the context of the need outlined, the strategy of the organization that is being addressed, and they should then ask what the best integrated method of implementing the solution is. This does not minimize the authority or purpose of management. It acknowledges the realization that the complexity of change and the best methods of implementation may not be short in duration. This task may be better executed in a manner that addresses the stated need and prepares for several other needs that may have been identified in the past or by other parts of the organization. The view of solutions at the level of the implementer can be different and tactically better within the context of the macrostrategy.

As an example, the company determines that its direct sales force and manufacturing processes are effective but that incremental benefit can be achieved by establishing relationships with distributors. Distributors would reach into market segments that are not currently served, but the lower margins of these sales would still benefit the organization by spreading costs over increased volume and adding no increases to fixed expenses. An interesting truth about software is that it bends to meet the purpose it serves. Over time, small and large changes are made to meet the primary purpose and focus of the tasks it supports. This is just like a builder of log houses who, over time, develops employees who are very good at construction. The builder acquires the tools needed, develops relationships with vendors, builds institutional knowledge about the tasks, and develops an ability to predict the types and nature of possible obstacles that might negatively affect the building of log houses. The processes of entering data, building reports, structuring customer data, standardizing methods of billing, among others, are honed to meet the needs of these primary functions. If I were told to strategically alter the business model to include the use of distributors, I would propose that some new key structures be built to support the identity of the distributors, interactions with them, and their impact on the overall business. If I were told that the organization would develop some relationships with distributors and needed to have information associated with these activities available in a rapid manner, I would propose something very different from my previous response because it was not presented as a strategic change in the business model. Often these types of changes are presented as a "test" for the organization and the ability to show data about this test needs to be executed to prove the pros and cons of the concept. Of course, the solutions and methods used to implement the test solution are viewed as work done, and additional work is built on this poor foundation.

The log house builder might decide to also build brick houses using this same approach. A new brick house would be built, and it would likely suffer from issues that an experienced brick house builder would have learned to avoid over time. These scenarios also take place within organizations, and building on weak technical foundations will always create incrementally more work

and complexity than a structurally well-designed and implemented solution. The fundamental lesson is that there are no
short cuts to building new strategies and coming up with technical solutions for those strategies. Information technology and its
many tentacles are now foundational in nature, and are as critical
as the ideas and strategies they are asked to support.

Chapter Six

Technology Gaps within the Organization Will be Filled Intentionally or Unintentionally

———— ※※※※※※※※※※※※ ————

When different segments of the business bring in technology, without support from their own information technology (IT) group, and start to use it within the company, it indicates that there is some type of gap in the technology infrastructure. No longer is there any technology that does not have additional implications for the entire organization and for IT. There needs to be an overarching understanding of how new technology will be paid for, how it will be supported, security implications, and how it integrates into the existing technology structure. Bring your own devices is a recent example of this concept.[31] The information

---

31 "Bring your own device...means the policy of permitting employees to bring personally owned mobile devices (laptops, tablets, and smart phones) to their workplace, and use those devices to access privileged company information and applications." Wikipedia, "Bring your own device," http://en.wikipedia.org/wiki/Bring_your_own_device

technology group needs to be the funnel for new technology into the organization. More important to note, however, is that new gadgets are not always good business tools.

Perhaps more than in any other area of the organization, the phrase "A solution looking for a problem" is most often a valid statement. People become enamored of some technology presented to the organization or introduced to the greater society, and they read about the efficiencies and improvements it can bring to an organization. The technology fever is best exemplified by the bust of the technology bubble.[32] For a period, there was an assumption that any business model that became Internet based was going to be the new and dominant solution for the consumers of that business model. The lessons of the technology bubble's bust are well documented, so it is the internalization of that lesson on a practical level of technology management that I will address here.

In large and small businesses, it is not unusual for individuals to obtain technology in the form of software, hardware, or databases to meet specific needs not addressed by the larger IT organization. Employees, when faced with a need to achieve an objective that cannot or will not be resolved by the larger organization within a required time frame, will try to find a path that will achieve the objective with the resources they have available. If it requires the purchase of software to be placed on someone's business computer, then some very interesting events have been set in motion. Someone will learn how to use this software to some level of expertise. Some business time will be spent utilizing the software to achieve the objective of the purchase. The

---

32   "The dot-com bubble (also referred to as the dot-com boom, the Internet bubble and the information technology bubble) was a speculative bubble covering roughly 1997–2000...during which stock markets in industrialized nations saw their equity value rise rapidly from growth in the Internet sector and related fields. While the latter part was a boom and bust cycle, the Internet boom is sometimes meant to refer to the steady commercial growth of the Internet with the advent of the World Wide Web, as exemplified by the first release of the Mosaic web browser in 1993, and continuing through the 1990s. The period was marked by the founding (and, in many cases, spectacular failure) of a group of new Internet-based companies commonly referred to as *dot-coms*. Companies were seeing their stock prices shoot up if they simply added an "e-" prefix to their name and/or a ".com" to the end, which one author called "prefix investing". Wikipedia, "Dot-Com Bubble," http://en.wikipedia.org/wiki/Dot-com_bubble.

greater IT organization may or may not know of the existence of the software, and it may violate some established policies related to nonstandard organizational software existing on company computers. The resulting solution may or may not require continued use of the software, and it may or may not be able to be integrated into the greater software and data structures established by the organization. Since I have done this myself, I can attest to the very strong belief that these actions were correct and benefited the organization, even with the divergence from a larger IT strategy and budget. Whether it was software, hardware, or consultants that were used in this scenario, the relevant organizational topics are:

- There was a real or perceived need to achieve an objective that the larger IT group could not or would not address within a specific time frame.
- Resources, both financial and human, were used to achieve an IT objective but were not part of the larger IT budget model or strategic plan.
- A solution that may or may not be needed on an ongoing basis was generated and represents something of real or perceived value to the organization.

I view this as an island of capability, knowledge, information, and risk for the organization. Risk is one of the most interesting aspects of these types of activities. Risk can be broken down into several pieces.

1. The ad-hoc nature of a solution may generate data or information that is useful in answering a narrowly defined question but can generate misleading or erroneous information when viewed in the context of the larger

organization.[33] A non-IT example of data or information being useful but misleading if not viewed from a holistic view is an experience I had in Taiwan. We were performing a clinical analysis of the presence of pressure ulcers, for the first time in Taiwan, to understand the scope and value of introducing preventative products. We translated English-based surveys, utilized translators to explain the process, and collected the data manually into spreadsheets. We measured the number of patients with pressure ulcers and the departments where the patients resided. We determined if the pressure ulcers existed prior to admission to a hospital or developed while there. The numbers presented a good argument for the introduction of preventative products. Because of previous experiences and the general unknown nature of the health care process in Taiwan, we asked additional questions about the admission process and how patients came to be in the various departments of the hospital. After some time, we learned that the vast majority of patients entered the hospital through a specific staging area. They tended to be in this area for at least an hour, and many patients were placed on very hard surfaces until moved into the other departments. After additional analysis, we determined that it was this process that was the source of the majority of the pressure ulcers developed by patients, but the issue — because it took time to present as a problem — was not determined until these patients resided in other departments. This was not Sherlock Holmes–level analysis and discovery, but it does demonstrate how — in the absence of rigorous review — data can be collected and presented while still not communicating the entire cause-and-effect story.

---

33   "The terms data, information and knowledge are frequently used for overlapping concepts. The main difference is in the level of abstraction being considered. Data is the lowest level of abstraction, information is the next level, and finally, knowledge is the highest level among all three." Wikipedia, "Data – Meaning of data, information and knowledge," http://en.wikipedia.org/wiki/Data

2. The repeatability of the process may require more extensive periods of time. This can create a situation in which the results are useful but take too long to generate and be of ongoing value. One of the tenets of IT is generating results that the organization can effectively use and within a reasonable period of time. When non-IT professionals generate ad-hoc solutions, it is common for these types of tenets not to be considered. I greatly value creativity, but there are considerations that IT professionals evaluate, as a standard part of solution development, that non-IT professionals consider roadblocks. Because ad-hoc solutions are intentionally done outside IT organization, the value of the solution can suffer from maladies that IT-supported activities would not.

3. A narrow solution is created for what is truly a larger-process issue that should be addressed by a more robust solution.

4. These negatives cloud the true potential nature of the work performed. More energy is spent on explaining why the process was not correct, and less time is spent on the purpose, the results, and the reason why it was done outside of the IT organization.

Media and technology publications present the newest and sexiest technology because that is what it is believed people want to see and brings their eyes to media products. Such publications create conversation within organizations that may adopt new technology in the hope of creating a competitive advantage that leads to revenue. But sexy is not equal to opportunity, opportunity is not equal to need, and need is not equal to purchasing. This is where some of the pressure to adopt technology is generated. There is something new in the marketplace, and it could be the incremental tool that makes your business better than someone else's, or are you left falling behind your competitors because they have decided to move forward with new technology. Whatever the case, these types of pressure help bring outside technology into organizations. No matter how much or little the processes change, it can be such change that truly drives the acceptance or rejection of technology. The linkage between new technology and process cannot be broken. Determining if the process change associated with technology is also of value is not always linked as directly as needed to fully understand the impact of that technology. The process changes introduced by adopting an enterprise resource planning (ERP) system are significant, and the definition of success is not only having the software work but having the software *and* new processes work. Implementing a faster network may appear to be a non-process type of change, but it brings the ability to accomplish tasks faster and opportunities to adopt new processes that these faster speeds allow. These new processes may, for example, include streaming Internet music to desktops rather than the intended purpose of the change. Managing the processes — both intended and unintended — brought by new technology is a true challenge.

A recent example of how process changes brought by new technology can be resisted — because of the implications of the technology and not its inherent value — can be found in the book (and subsequent movie) *Moneyball*[34] which highlights the resistance of consummate baseball professionals who resisted the analytical approach of their general manager because it took out the "gut" feelings of scouts from the equation.

Because of the constant bombardment of new and different technology, setting strategic objectives and then executing those objectives over three- or five-year windows is very difficult. The saying "hindsight is 20/20" is a constant obstacle for IT professionals. Decisions have to be made on what is known and assumed, and this has to be preserved so it can be referenced to answer the inevitable question, why did you make that choice?

---

34   Michael Lewis, *Moneyball: The Art of Winning an Unfair Game* (New York: Norton, 2003); a film based on the book, directed by Bennett Miller and starring Brad Pitt, was released in 2011.

My thought process about technology has evolved to include a few basic criteria.

- What does any technology bring in the way of opportunity to the business in the areas of cost reduction, cost avoidance, efficiency, or competitive advantage relative to what is currently in place? Drop all the hyperboles and focus on the raw facts that impact your real business.
- There are no magic bullets. There is no software, hardware, or consultant that will change your cost or revenue model so dynamically that you must react rather than assess and fine-tune the strategic plan already in place.
- Trends are large numbers of people agreeing that something has changed in the existing models and warrants attention. Determining if that change requires your organization to react is never clear. The horse and buggy was replaced by the automobile. If you defined yourself as a maker of buggies, then you eventually closed your business. If you defined yourself as being in the transportation business, you started a taxi service.

Information technology is unique in its ability to be introduced into an organization at many different levels and by purely non-IT individuals. The marketing department is not going to bring a new e-mail software package into the organization but may bring a three-user statistical package in to crunch numbers that the IT organization indicated it could not address at that moment. Some may call this a creative solution or describe this as a sign of being nimble within the larger organization.

This type of event shows a gap within the organization that needs to be addressed. One point of view could be that the strategic planning processes did not correctly address the need for statistical analysis and that the business is reacting to the void. Another point of view may be that the IT department does not possess skills that the business now requires and thus must obtain them to meet the needs of the organization. It also could show that a new hire entered the company with these type of skills and sold the marketing department vice president on the benefits that could be gained from having these skills utilized within the department. Whatever the reason, a non-IT-based group has spent money and human time on a tool that may or may not be best suited to achieving the objective and that may not scale to an organizational level, and results may or may not represent the answer needed because the input, process, and methods used may not have accessed the correct or all the available resources.

The saying "It's better to beg for forgiveness than to ask for permission" fits this scenario, and I have been guilty of taking this path in the past. When departments, resources, and IT were not as closely intertwined and the scope of data was not as vast, these types of activities would not be as limited in value. The bottom line is that unless the capabilities of the software, the knowledge of the user, the source of the data, the value to the organization, and the time spent are placed within the context of the larger organization the entire effort may be a total waste of time and resources.

Today's reality is that IT needs to assume that opportunities may arise that departments feel are strong enough to warrant spending money and time on. If IT does not plan on these events occurring, it will likely be viewed as a barrier to creativity and nimble responsiveness. If the IT plan included execution of several "proof of concepts" during the plan period, and a structure was built through which management could be presented the opportunities and explanation of the benefits and costs, a process would be in place to bring forward these ideas, and the skills and knowledge of organization could be brought into the effort. If the internal resources are not available, the organization may decide to provide resources in excess of the ones available to the department and have outside resources execute the task. The key concept is to understand that the unknown will create these types of situations and that there is a path that they can follow. If IT is locked into just the plan, the tasks outlined in the plan, and cannot react to dynamics of today's organizations, it will be viewed as a barrier to innovation and responsiveness.

An example of how internal ideas can be developed within an organization is a consulting project for a very large manufacturer in North Carolina. This company supported creativity internally by asking for ideas that could benefit the company and potentially become revenue centers instead of just cost centers. A group that supported the preventative maintenance of one the company's multi-acre manufacturing facilities believed that a software package could be developed that would better track and schedule the many activities required to prevent or react to mechanical failures that would interrupt production lines. The company had a process for soliciting ideas, and providing real resources to ideas, that internal employees believed had value.

It is difficult to identify ideas that do not have an IT component or would not benefit from IT input. Information technology is a vital part of the organization process, and ideas will always come into play that can benefit some or all aspects of the organization. Not managing these ideas within the IT discipline limits their ability to be successful — and to their benefiting the larger organization. Information technology must and should be more than an executer of tasks; it needs to be a promoter, facilitator, and executor of tasks. The IT infrastructure needs to be given the ability to support and help direct IT activities that are brought into the organization so that the full opportunity of these activities can be utilized.

Chapter Seven

Small or Large, Your Philosophy about Technology Should Remain the Same

What are the internal resources that make your business competitive, profitable, and unique? Owning an information technology (IT) structure is a lot like owning or renting a home. When you rent and problems occur with the home, you call someone to correct them; that is one reason you pay money to someone else to provide you a home. When you own your own home and problems occur, you determine if you or someone else will correct the problem. Renters have some, but far fewer, responsibilities than homeowners — and *responsibilities* is the key word.

If I started a company from scratch today, I would strongly consider operating as a virtual company. I would have an outsourced telephone system, which would likely entail voice over

Internet protocol,[35] e-mail, a website, and software and disk storage. Being an IT person who has written and implemented software, I believe that whatever business I would start should not
be impacted by any issues related to the moving parts of IT. What
do I mean by the "moving parts"? I would want my company to
optimize the value of IT but not have to deal with actually running it.

Let's break this down into individual parts.

Telephony is a vital aspect of any business. The way people
perceive your business is based on how the communication process works when a phone call is placed. Utilization of a professional person, and not an electronic interface, or IVR,[36] tells me
something about an organization. I have been impressed by the
evolution of voice recognition software and how much better it
has become at understanding words and phrases. Despite this
fact, I know that there is no way to anticipate or to expect people
communicating with a start-up company to explain the purpose
of their call to a computer. Yes, such systems are cost-efficient,
may replace full-time employees, and can handle volume changes in calls, but would I leave the communication process of my
start-up business to a computer? I may have given the hosting
of the technology and the physical hardware to an another company, but I would want to own the physical communication. I
would have IVR software in place for those situations in which a
human could not be present, but the majority of communication
would involve real people. I have found that more companies
have made access to people very difficult and, in some cases, I
have not found any way to contact a human representative. If
a start-up company is receiving more calls than one person can

35   "Voice over IP (VoIP, or voice over Internet Protocol) commonly refers to the communication pro-
      tocols, technologies, methodologies, and transmission techniques involved in the delivery of voice
      communications and multimedia sessions over Internet Protocol (IP) networks, such as the Inter-
      net." Mashable, "Voip," http://mashable.com/category/voip/.

36   "Interactive voice response (IVR) is a technology that allows a computer to interact with humans
      through the use of voice and DTMF [dual-tone multifrequency] tones input via keypad." Wikipe-
      dia, "Interactive voice response," http://en.wikipedia.org/wiki/IVR

handle correctly, either things are going really well or very badly. In either case, determine the topics of the calls and then determine if some of them are basic enough for IVR; if so, patch them through to IVR. Yes, if people know they can get to a human they will avoid IVR software. After obtaining a good track record of the type of calls and the topics that are discussed, having one layer of IVR in place before the caller reaches a human representative would likely benefit those on both sides of the phone call. People do learn that basic questions can be handled by nonhumans; they simply want the option of human response available.

An example of simply not understanding what a consumer needs and following a process that sounds good on paper but in reality is a business killer was a support call I placed with a vendor regarding my inability to gain access to download software updates. Putting aside the irony of calling support about how to gain the correct access to their own support site, I needed to understand how to use their online support site to gain access to software we owned. I went to the site and, after searching every path I could find, could not find a method to contact a living person. I determined that access to humans was not allowed as a first step in the process. I found an e-mail address to send my request for assistance and provided all my contact information. I had expected a response by phone, but received an e-mail outlining what some person thought was the answer to my question, but with no way of phoning anyone in response. Over the next three days, I continued to receive e-mails that did not address my problem and continued to have no access to a human, despite my requests to have an ear-to-ear conversation. On the third day I reached my limit; I sent an e-mail that in part said, "In the name of all things holy, do not send me any more e-mails. Call me and allow me to explain what I need. Show me mercy." I did receive a call as a result of this e-mail. Someone considered this method of support effective and, no doubt, cost-effective, but I was not against dropping use of the software. There are cases when people have told me they would rather not interact with support and deal with a software problem themselves, despite having a service contract. In no reality is this an acceptable model, yet it happens.

E-mail is now a commodity service and need. To spend money on maintaining e-mail software and hardware is difficult to justify. My wife runs two nonprofit organizations, and I recently helped move both organizations to a hosted e-mail service. As with many nonprofits, their business is providing programming, services, and fund-raising. Having someone who is capable of supporting an e-mail server and software has nothing to do with their business model. Customer relationship management (CRM) software can still be leveraged, and providers like Google can deal with the mechanics of e-mail. Of course, a hosted system provides access to e-mail for any device and from any location.

Much like e-mail, websites have become more of a commodity but you have to determine if your website is strategic enough to bother owning. I cannot imagine Amazon not controlling all aspects of its website. Amazon provides hosting for websites, takes the mechanics of hardware out of the equation, and lets users maintain their own sites. The basic question remains the same: Is control of the physical and software parts of your website critical to your business model? Even with hosted sites, integration with customer relationship management (CRM) software can be achieved. The amazing aspects of the web are that, small or large, a company or organization can have a compelling and integrated website to support its business model. Having created some websites, I will say that working with large providers reduces the risks associated with smaller firms. In the past, I worked with smaller hosting companies and found over time that the short-term benefits did not outweigh the security and cost benefits of the larger providers.

Computer networks present a more complicated issue than the previous topics discussed. If you utilize a voice over Internet protocol system, there are additional complications associated with a network. To outsource all aspects of network hardware, software, and data storage can be expensive. If your business is related to networks, then clearly owning your network is not a difficult model. If you are a nonprofit with ten employees, your network is far outside your area of focus. If you grow large enough, the cost model of having internal resources to support a network may become substantial enough to justify the transition. If you are able to have a totally virtual company that has no central office, then these specific challenges do not need to be addressed.

Software can be the most complicated topic to address, but you need to maintain a clear understanding of what your business is and where you want to use your human resources. As mentioned earlier, I am a big believer in optimizing all aspects of any software owned or utilized. You do not need your ERP software to be in your office, running on your computer, and maintained by your employees to leverage functionality and derive value. Licensing, support, upgrades, patches, time zones, segregation of duties, and integration with other software products need to be considered. Dealing with outsourced providers is a job in itself. The desire to reach through the phone line and shake a representative until he or she understand the point you are making does occur, and when it does it challenges your belief in having chosen this path. However, the challenges of owning the same processes yourself will provide these same type of moments.

The ability to outsource file storage is fairly new, and the technology press talks a great deal about the concept of "big data."[37] Other than the people who work in your organization, data are what makes what you do unique. Data are stored and then accessed to fulfill the concept of taking data to information and then to knowledge. The structure of data is discussed in chapter 12.

---

37   " Big data is a collection of data sets so large and complex that it becomes difficult to process using on-hand database management tools or traditional data processing applications. The challenges include capture, curation, storage, search, sharing, transfer, analysis, and visualization. The trend to larger data sets is due to the additional information derivable from analysis of a single large set of related data, as compared to separate smaller sets with the same total amount of data, allowing correlations to be found to 'spot business trends, prevent diseases, combat crime.'" Wikipedia, "Big data," http://en.wikipedia.org/wiki/Big_data

Why are data second only to people? The answer can be found in the words said by customers when speaking to call centers, to salespeople, and in focus groups or when writing on blogs. If this information is stored, it is likely on disks and in unstructured data, comments in orders, recorded call center conversations, and customer comments. Again, where do you want your resources to be used in performing your business? The mechanics of data storage, backups, performance tuning, and retention are incredibly important and vital to any organization. If you believe that your business is unique in executing its tasks and brings value that others do not or cannot, you will want to link these processes to your customers and strategically note this uniqueness. If the focus is on obtaining knowledge from your data, and the mechanics are more of a commodity, then your resources may be analytical and you may have others perform the storage aspects. Once again, this is not an act of minimizing the value of maintaining an effective data structure or of database administrators (DBAs).[38] DBAs have enabled me to have an effective role in analysis. When I run into the barriers of multilayered queries and pushing the limits of database analysis, DBAs help me get things to run faster and better. It is the physical mechanics of disk storage and not the bending of the data structures to provide value that is being outsourced.

There are so many different types of models that can be considered. You can outsource all aspects of your technology infrastructure but have internal resources perform the analytics against your data. I believe that the key components of any business are the strategic functions and analysis of the past, present, and future data of the organization. Establishing the direction and providing nongeneric analysis of the business is not something easily done by non-internal resources. Yes, an organization may bring in consultants to perform these types of functions, but

---

38   "A database administrator (short form DBA) is a person responsible for the installation, configuration, upgrade, administration, monitoring and maintenance of databases in an organization." Wikipedia, "Database Administrator," http://en.wikipedia.org/wiki/Database_administrator.

the execution, insights, and measurements remain part of the internal resources of the organization. My work as a consultant generated the best results when I took my skill sets and knowledge and integrated them into the software and processes of a particular organization. For a short time, I learned the organization's processes; then I took their uniqueness and gave them physical presence.

In no way am I minimizing the importance or value of people performing with quality the tasks I have outlined as part of outsourcing. The ability to have them function with 99.99 percent availability and make them basically transparent to the organization requires skills and dedication to those functions. It is a determination of which skills you require your business model to own and which ones you might choose to rent. They are all important. Obviously, as your organization grows, the cost benefit of bringing external resources in-house change, but your philosophy about how and why you use these technologies should not. I will end where I started, by saying that small or large, your philosophy about technology should stay the same.

Chapter Eight

There Is Always a Past, Present, and Future

———⎯⎯⎯⎯⎯⎯⎯⎯⎯⎯⎯⎯———

The past tells you what you have done; the present tells you where you are now, and it will soon be the past. The future is what you are shaping with the past and present. The skeleton of every organization is based on the people and structures that were built to sustain the organization but are much harder to change than strategies and goals for the future. Changing the physical structure of databases to reflect a new or modified strategy is much harder than changing the strategy.

I have experienced corporate restructuring, process changing, and rethinking of business with consultants. People always change, processes change in varying degrees, and some data collected may change. Even when entirely new software is introduced, it is rare to have the foundational data structures, which are the data skeleton of the organization, change in a meaningful manner. The business rules that created the data tables, the strategy that was in place when the data structures were created, and the business model that was present at the outset may have all changed, but changing the core data structures of the organization is very hard work. Making true change and adding true flexibility to your organization should include the painful process of examining and restructuring the data to provide what is needed by the changes made in processes and people.

In the world of information technology (IT), the changes taking place in the costs and capabilities of hardware and software are so dynamic that decisions made today can be challenged in less than five years if those who do the challenging do not understand the capabilities and limits of the technology at the time the decision was made. I spoke of the skeleton above. The skeleton of every organization is the foundational aspects of information buried in the core data structures that the organization creates and maintains. It is difficult to overvalue the importance of these core data structures and the massive downstream impact these values have on every activity and on the analyses performed each day.

I have an accounting background, so I will use a chart of accounts as an example of something that organizations do not review and reevaluate as often as they do marketing strategies and management structures. Oddly, it is easier to change marketing strategies and management than to change the nature of charts of accounts and customer data tables.[39] Unfortunately, people and businesses think of these structures as rigid, remaining basically the same year after year. People, processes, and the world keep changing, but these structures are often thought of as maintaining

---

39   "A chart of accounts (COA) is a created list of the accounts used by a business entity to define each class of items for which money or the equivalent is spent or received. It is used to organize the finances of the entity and to segregate expenditures, revenue, assets and liabilities in order to give interested parties a better understanding of the financial health of the entity. The list can be numerical, alphabetical, or alpha-numeric. The structure and headings of accounts should assist in consistent posting of transactions. Each nominal ledger account is unique to allow its ledger to be located. The list is typically arranged in the order of the customary appearance of accounts in the financial statements, balance sheet accounts followed by profit and loss accounts." Wikipedia, "Chart of accounts," http://en.wikipedia.org/wiki/Chart_of_accounts

their form because they are not considered to have an impact on or be as meaningful to a business. This is not true.

When a business starts, a chart of accounts is built to reflect the financial measurements that are required for internal and external reporting of results at a specific point in time. Without going into a very boring explanation of how a chart of accounts can be constructed, these sequence of numbers (e.g., 1000 = Assets, or 1000-200-697 = Bank of America account) represent the thoughts and beliefs of the individuals who determined their structure and the subsequent reporting that would be generated from the numbers stored in these values. If you view these values as static numbers that change infrequently and that changes in the world would not significantly impact how these values should be viewed, then selecting a structure of (1000-1234) instead of this structure (100000-12345-4566-123) would not be viewed as a critical decision among the many other decisions that always need to be made.[40] It is unlikely that Bill Gates or Michael Dell knew how their business would grow and evolve or what the ideal chart of accounts would be for a business ten years after it started. Moving from small to medium to large is easier because changes to the skeleton of data structures are forced by new software, hardware, and processes, but once the larger status is reached, large-scale changes to software, hardware, and processes becomes an option that is balanced among needs for public reporting, internal processes, and financial reporting. The thought process utilized to create the chart of accounts five years prior may only reflect 50 percent of the nature of the business that currently exists. I am not saying that the chart of accounts cannot present the current cash position, the total sales, or the liabilities of the organization. I am saying that the chart may have incorporated all the products that the company sold and the processes required to sell those

---

40   In the first figure, 1000 indicates an asset-type item, and 1234 indicates that it is a bank account. In the second figure, 100000 indicates an asset, but there can be many more than 1000 allows; 12345 indicates a bank account, but there can by many more than 1234; 4566 indicates the type of asset (e.g., a CD), and 123 gives it a geographical identity for tax implications.

products, like commissions and the cost to manufacture. More important, the people in the organization developed analysis models using the chart of accounts to understand the changes in the key aspects of the business and trend these data over time. Five years later, there are many more products, the method of selling has added distributors, the market segments have changed, and another company was purchased. This chart of account value 1000-1234 provided the granularity required previously but now it is limited, by its very structure, to provide the granularity and flexibility that this value 100000-12345-4566-123 can provide. There are limits to what type of reporting should and can be provided from the chart of accounts, but it is integrated into many other ancillary data structures like sales, accounts receivable, payables, orders, and the like. It is this integration that cannot be changed without serious thought and resources, and thus it becomes less likely to be addressed. Frankly, it is easier and sexier to say you are changing the marketing and strategy because it *is* easier, and restructuring the chart of accounts sounds like tactical work. In fact, the inability to correctly align strategy to the chart of accounts will cause endless workarounds and wasted resources.

As an example, the 4000 range of the chart of accounts represents the product revenue of the company. Individuals in the organization use these values to track the revenue; it was the best and most accurate way of generating these data and was less complicated than using the sales order data. It is hard to underestimate the number of work hours and thought that goes into generating not only reports but individual spreadsheets and personalized views of the business. Not sometimes, not maybe, but always these actions take place. The historical inherent rigidity of the chart of accounts and the knowledge that changes require real effort and time make such changes almost an "act of God." I would argue that any organization that does not have these types of activities taking place is either nearly perfect or lacks individuals who want more and better information. In addition, reports rightly or wrongly assume that the maximum size of the chart of accounts is the space that needs to be reserved and that the other space is filled up with other data. Increasing the size of the chart of accounts also may require that reports be modified, that logic used to strip apart 1000-1234 will differ greatly from that used to strip apart 100000-12345-4566-123. Individuals create from what they already have and know. After a thousand work hours are put into the structural reports and standardized reporting, changing these structures becomes a significant challenge and is sometimes not fully appreciated or understood by the organization.

Once an organization has reached a size that requires reporting to other legal entities and structurally has groups of people managing the accounting functions, changes to data structures like the chart of accounts are difficult and costly because of the number of legal and structural changes that must be considered. The first standard reaction is to create a "work-around." Some report may move to the sales order structure because it has the more granular data wanted, but others may stay with the chart of accounts. As with any accounting system there are transactions, like journal entries,[41] that do not have corresponding entries in the sales order tables. Now data come from two sources that differ in function and actual data points. This is the beginning of having multiple possible answers to questions that are technically the same, yet the different sources can produce different answers. The nuances of generating these types of reports and the lack of transparency and understanding of end consumers of these data is the beginning of complexity and ultimately confusion. Users will always find ways to obtain the data they require and will not wait for management or the IT department to generate better information. This is the unintended consequence of not focusing on the structures that provide the best information

---

41   "A journal entry, in accounting, is a logging of transactions into accounting journal items. The journal entry can consist of several items, each of which is either a debit or a credit." Wikipedia, "Journal entry," http://en.wikipedia.org/wiki/Journal_entry

or the desired data, and "kicking the data can down the road." The accounting group may advocate for not adding complexity to the chart of accounts for maintenance and control reasons. The organization needs to consciously choose and indicate where the best source of specific types of data exist and what business rules apply to each option.

This discussion may appear a bit obscure in nature but presents one of the most important concepts of IT philosophy. Knowing that the core data structures are the skeleton of the information structures of your organization should cause them to be more ro-bust than is currently required and to be created with the future in mind. If maximum flexibility is established as a requirement, despite what many will call overkill, there will be flexibility built into the data skeleton and, more importantly, it will be respon-sive to the needs of the consumers. If a new company asked me to implement its new accounting system, I would have a chart of ac-counts that looked like 100000-12345-4566-123; the first customer number would be 100000 so all reports have the same number of characters, and there would be a large range for growth. The customer file would have unused character, date, and numeric fields that could contain data points when new functionality is needed. There would be the ability for multitier pricing and other growth-enabling structures that have maintenance screens that can be controlled by the users. Reports would be built to already have these data points available to present. It is always easier to build a new house with the features you want today and might want tomorrow than it will be to modify the house later. It is vastly easier to build in functionality in the beginning than after processes and time have established patterns that users can rely on and expect.

Establishing this future functionality addresses the needs of the present and future. The past, of course, also requires atten-tion. Starting to use new data fields and adding functionality may require that all elements of the table be updated, including a new customer field. But some fields may apply to the nature of a transactional record, like an order, and then it is important to determine what the past orders will or will not contain in this field. As I indicated earlier, having nothing, or null, in a field indicates nothing to anyone. It indicates that nothing is present but not that a conscious decision was made to leave it null. I would populate the field with a value that indicates it was "stubbed" with a nonmeaningful value; meaningful values will, over time, become the dominant values. In the old days, when disk space was expensive and processing speeds were a fraction of those available today, this approach would have been expensive and inappropriate. Not in today's world.

Over time, management, department personnel, processes, strategies, and knowledge about the past will change, but the data will live on for many more years. It is the legacy and past nature of the organization; in many ways, it is the archeological history of the organization. When organizations speak of losing institutional knowledge of employees, part of that knowledge is the what, why, and how of the core skeleton data. One of the great failures of corporate acquisitions is not to understand and retain the skeleton data of an acquired organization. Just as key employees are valuable, the understanding of what skeleton data points are critical to making that organization unique from others is vital. I have seen successful organizations purchased and taken away from their core skeleton data structures and incorporated into existing systems for efficiency and justification of cost savings. Once these organizations realize that they cannot obtain the information they expect in the manner they expect, business falters and "fire fights" are put into place to re-create the same data that were once among the unique and valuable assets of the organization.

Chapter Nine

Who is going to do the work?

———— \\\\\\\\\\\\\\\\\\\\\\\\\\\\ ————

Not long ago, I read an article titled "GM's U-Turn" in
InformationWeek[42] It highlights that General Motors (GM) was
going to go from 90 percent outsourced and 10 percent insourced
to 90 percent insourced and 10 percent outsourced. This is significant for many reasons, but I want to focus on two topics.

First, outsourcing was a way to cut costs, improve efficiency,
and establish cost controls, among other perceived benefits. The
information technology (IT) magazines wrote about outsourcing
every day, and the concept reached every executive group and
company board. If you considered IT a commodity and thought
its functions were not as strategic as new product development or
marketing, then having people in India writing code and having
some individuals manage the process within your organization
resulted in cost-saving and other benefits to your organization.
The company Electronic Data Systems became the outsourced IT

---

42   Chris Murphy, "GM's U-Turn," *InformationWeek*, July 9, 2012.

for GM,[43] and was in fact owned by GM for a period of time. Once the fad was well established, the less appealing aspects of outsourcing and well-documented failures began to be featured in the very same publications that had brought outsourcing to the consciousness of the public.

Of course, not all outsourcing has failed or will end. What GM has determined is that "When the business says 'go,' that means we start working on a contract, we don't start working on a project." The fundamental concept here is that IT needs to be responsive and strategic, and an outsourced human group does not fit that model. It is important to note that outsourcing had its origins at a time when the hardware and human resources of IT were more expensive and the Internet had not yet brought its transformational impact to the world. This does not alter the fact that the human aspect of IT is not a commodity and institutional knowledge, ownership, and development of IT processes are likely to be more effective than an outsourced version of these human processes. This is the difference between the physical layers discussed in chapter seven.

Second, IT is subject to fads like every other business process. Concepts are presented, the short-term benefits of actions are hailed in the media, and some companies take actions that appear to make them better able to compete. As mentioned previously, anyone who has had to make a support call and reached an outsourced support group — and after the call thought about how to avoid the company and its support group in the future — should question the true benefit of outsourcing. Alienation of customers will never be beneficial to any organization, and short-term benefits that cause long-term problems — and, ultimately, additional

---

43   "Electronic Data Systems (EDS) was an American multinational information technology equipment and services company headquartered in Plano, Texas. It was established in 1962 by H. Ross Perot. Perot's goal was to start a company that offered skilled electronic data processing management personnel along with the computer equipment. He targeted large corporations and offered long-term contracts at a time when short-term contracts were the norm. In 1984, General Motors agreed to buy EDS for $2.5 billion. In 1996, GM spun off EDS as an independent company and became one of its largest clients." Wikipedia, "Electronic Data System," http://en.wikipedia.org/wiki/Electronic_Data_Systems

costs—do not benefit anyone. If you outsource your telephony process, it does not mean that internal resources should not learn and understand all features and functions of the system so that strategic decisions can be made based on the full capabilities of the telephony tool. Today, outsourcing should not mean loss of the strategic knowledge needed to leverage the tool but that the majority of the physical aspects of the technology are managed by individuals who can optimize that portion of the technology. Strategic full-time equivalents (FTEs[44]) may not be the individuals who upgrade the software and hardware of the telephony system, but they are the ones who understand how to make it work within the strategic framework of the organization. Of course, you will hear that the outsourcer can also provide this capability. That is possible, but my experience indicates that outsourced resources are never aligned and retained over time like an internal resource. Learning how an organization uses any technology and understanding the nuances is critical to the organization. George Santayana's famous expression "Those who cannot remember the past are condemned to repeat it" is as true for IT as it is for anything else. There are few IT decisions that do not consider a multitude of moving parts before determining a course of action. This decision matrix indicates why the level of granularity and processes were implemented and how it was intended to be used by the organization.

What is this "thing" that IT people bring and acquire in a business over time? What knowledge and capabilities are valuable enough to want to retain? I have outlined some of these answers in previous chapters, yet sports has a wealth of examples to draw upon. The Boston Celtics played on the parquet floors of the Boston Garden, and it has been said that players like Larry Bird knew the dead spots and could use that knowledge to their advantage. Knowing this type of information is not related to a

---

44   "Full-time equivalent (FTE) is a unit that indicates the workload of an employed person (or student) in a way that makes workloads comparable across various contexts." Wikipedia, "Full-time equivalent," http://en.wikipedia.org/wiki/Full-time_equivalent

player's physical skills or the rules of basketball; it is very specific information about the nature of the space and is acquired over time and through experience. Did this knowledge win games for the Boston Celtics? I do not know, but with all other factors in a playoff game being equal, I would want my team to know this information. Now, replace the parquet floor with your business and Larry Bird with your IT group. As mentioned previously, many businesses have the same software, hardware, and customers. The unique aspects and philosophy of your organization are the same as the soft spots on the parquet floor; it is local information acquired over time that presents opportunity to leverage something to your advantage.

There is a way of thinking that makes some IT people creative resources within an organization. Having a background in analyzing how technology interacts with people and having an analytical approach to repeatedly resolving issues that have a cause and effect creates a unique set of skills. When these experiences take place using the core data of many functional groups and processes of an organization, you acquire the archeological history mentioned earlier. Not every IT position exposes everyone to all the data structures or processes of an organization. As with all functional groups, not all IT individuals are interested in or will attempt to learn more than is mentioned in their explicit job requirements. This is not a criticism or judgment but an observation acquired over time. I have been fortunate to learn the fundamentals of accounting, worked within various types of businesses, have written code, and have developed analytical data tools. When presented with a request about something that I do not know a great deal about, I seek out individuals who can make that work happen and read about topics that are relevant to the subject. Combine this with a willingness to listen to individuals explain why this organization and process is unique from the boilerplate version and you then know enough to start melding together something that answers both the standard and unique questions that might be asked by the organization.[45]

It is not unusual for me to receive a phone call from an individual who says that someone told them that I might be able to help them with a question for which they have been unable to obtain an answer. This is not magic. It is an understanding of the tools and data available and how they can be leveraged and structured to answer questions on business.

---

45   "In computer programming, boilerplate code or boilerplate is the term used to describe sections of code that have to be included in many places with little or no alteration." Wikipedia, "Boilerplate Code," https://en.wikipedia.org/wiki/Boilerplate_code.

Chapter Ten

End Users and Fear

———— ⁂ ————

The first inroads that software and information technology (IT) made were in accounting and finance. Having numbers crunched and tracked by software and hardware was an obvious business process in which efficiencies and cost savings could be achieved. This is why chief financial officers were the individuals who initially had responsibility for IT. Of course, IT came into other functional areas, but the linkage to accounting and finance was strong and logical. This is also where the experience of individuals being replaced by IT took root. At one time, I was someone who proofed the financial numbers typed on reports. I employed the "double tape" process, which meant using a calculator, with a paper output tape, to add up a series of numbers twice to confirm the same number was obtained each time and matched what was on a report. This was not my only activity, but it was an important one that took hours to execute. I would also do an analysis of the balances in an account by taking a computer printout and crossing out the lines that netted to zero. It was these tasks—and their incredibly boring nature—that generated my interest in the workings of IT.

The term *efficiency* has been linked to IT since IT's origins in the business world. This linkage is well deserved, and the impact has changed the nature and purpose of individuals in a relatively short period of time. Waves of efficiency had first been feared and then later accepted as standard operating procedures. The "low-hanging fruit" of efficiencies and personnel reductions have been achieved, and a baseline resource model of IT and those functions that use IT have been established. The residual fear and knowledge that each new IT-based software install and hardware upgrade is linked to a cost savings that includes fewer people is an unfortunate legacy that needs to be altered. As with all waves of changes, people learn to expect benefits from actions and expenditures, but new expectations need to be established.

There is a point at which the number of employees is correct and the work needs to be changed to use the existing personnel more effectively. *Knowledge worker* has become the popular term for an individual who consumes and leverages the information produced by software and systems now in place.[46] The term *analytics* has become popular in many IT publications, and is the next logical step in using the vast amounts of information generated by the new, leaner versions of organizations.[47] There is an assumption that the information the knowledge worker and analytics is using to create the answers is correct or that this information has followed the same pattern long enough to generate useful information. This brings me back to the data skeleton of an organization, and the archeological history of that data skeleton. It is very possible

---

46   What differentiates knowledge work from other forms of work is its primary task of "nonroutine" problem solving, which requires a combination of convergent, divergent, and creative thinking. See Wolfgang Reinhardt, Benedikt Schmidt, Peter Sloep, and Hendrik Drachsler, "Knowledge Worker Roles and Actions—Results of Two Empirical Studies," *Knowledge and Process Management* 18, no. 3 (2011): 150–74.

47   "Analytics is the discovery and communication of meaningful patterns in data. Especially valuable in areas rich with recorded information, analytics rely on the simultaneous application of statistics, computer programming and operations research to quantify performance. Analytics often favors data visualization to communicate insight." Wikipedia, "Analytics," http://en.wikipedia.org/wiki/Analytics

that the knowledge worker and analytical software need to have a knowledgeable individual review the current rules used to create data and adjust the older data to conform to these rules before optimum value can be leveraged.

Let's say, for example, that Company A buys Company B in 2012. They both manufacture and build widgets. Company A operated on a 4–4–5 calendar,[48] and Company B operated on a monthly calendar. Each company established differently how it calculated the standard cost associated with the products manufactured. When the companies merged, large amounts of text was written about the differences between the two companies and how they would be integrated in the coming six months. Two years later, a newly hired knowledge worker uses analytical software to understand purchase and sales patterns from the last four years. A fact about the sales department is that it always wants to make sales quotas work within the time frames in which they are measured. Company A had a 4–4–5 pattern, and the sales department arranged its sales to make the goals established on this calendar. The new combined company now uses a standard calendar-month cycle. Having worked with a 4–4–5 calendar, I can say that the patterns are very different and, not adjusting for differences, will reduce the value of analysis. The people who knew the standard costs of Company A are now gone, and the person doing the work today lacks the knowledge of the archeological history of that data skeleton. Results are generated, patterns are reviewed, and the normal management questions come back about why the variances of X, Y, and Z exist. For anyone who has not been asked these types of questions, I can say from experience that fear is one reaction because the data present variances

---

48   "The 4–4–5 calendar is a method of managing accounting periods. It is a common calendar structure for some industries, such as retail, manufacturing and the parking industry. The 4–4–5 calendar divides a year into 4 quarters. Each quarter has 13 weeks which are grouped into two 4-week 'months' and one 5-week 'month.' When a 4–4–5 calendar is in use, reports with month-by-month comparisons or trend over periods do not make sense because one month is 25% larger than the other two. However, you can still compare a period to the same period in the prior year, or use week by week data comparison." Wikipedia, "4-4-5 calendar," http://en.wikipedia.org/wiki/4-4-5_calendar

but the reason for the variances is buried in the archeological history of that data skeleton; obtaining that information in a limited time frame is difficult at best. So begins the endless cycle of analysis, information generation, questioning of the information generated, and the limited ability to generate answers.

There is an additional step that needs to be executed if the answers to these types of questions are to be determined or at least understood better, and that is to perform some forensic IT analysis on the data skeleton. The granular chart of account values of each organization needs to be reviewed and aligned in the best manner possible. Then the current rules used to create the standard cost of manufactured items needs to be applied and recalculated for the four-year period using the smallest time frame possible, such as a day. These values are then used to understand sales and costs over time and compared to the previously calculated values. If there is a well-known seasonal fluctuation that is common to widget sales, that needs to be accounted for by creating time-segmented groupings of information. The bottom line is that this additional work provides information that can answer the *why* question and provide better analytical results. But it does require time, effort, and individuals capable of doing the work.

It is this type of retrospective action that develops answers that go beyond the standard measures and ratios of today's businesses. Today, just about anyone can run the basic business ratios and compare the results of the two companies and say that a cost for Company A is greater than for Company B, but what does that tell anyone without understanding the reasons for the difference? I have stopped listening to financial networks that talk about the results of companies year over year when they fail to mention that year one fell during an economic recession and year two was a recover year. The report that sales improved and margins improved is not followed by an analysis of how costs were reduced or stable during the recession or how management dealt with the downturn by pushing smaller sales commissions or long-term sales contracts that were not in place previously.

Sound-bite business analysis is as useful as sound-bite political analysis; the context is lost, and important information lies below the now common information generated by all businesses.

Unless HAL 9000 becomes part of every business,[49] the concept that IT brings efficiencies that allow reductions in FTEs instead of evolving and changing the view of value, needs to change dramatically. The low-hanging fruit of IT efficiencies has been harvested. Now there are the harder and more complex questions and processes that need to be addressed and analyzed by tools and people that understand the present and past and know what the future requires. End users need to know that IT is not a replacement of people but an enhancement of capabilities that add value to an organization. Of course, some individuals do not adapt as well as others or respond to the rapid change in the tools that are used. At the same time, there needs to be an understanding that the previous experiences and knowledge of the organization can provide valuable context to information generated now and going forward. Information technology now has to aid in capturing the processes and business rules of an organization from year to year and allow insertion of this information into the analysis of the organization. Business rules buried in software or spreadsheets do not allow management to place the correct context on information provided. If everyone uses the same techniques of analysis and data dissection, how does Company A become better or faster than Company B? Of course, the need to have uniform methods of reporting results to the public and regulatory agencies is required, but the many footnotes placed in company 10-Q statements are used to try to explain what the generic information cannot explain.[50] The replacement of text with

---

49   "HAL 9000 is a character in Arthur C. Clarke's science fiction *Space Odyssey* series. The primary antagonist in *2001: A Space Odyssey*, HAL (Heuristically programmed Algorithmic computer) is an artificial intelligence that controls the systems of the *Discovery One* spacecraft and interacts with the ship's astronaut crew." Wikipedia, "HAL 9000," http://en.wikipedia.org/wiki/HAL_9000.

50   "Form 10-Q shall be used for quarterly reports under Section 13 or 15(d) of the Securities Exchange Act of 1934 (15 U.S.C. 78m or 78o(d)), filed pursuant to Rule 13a-13 (17 CFR 240.13a-13) or Rule 15d-13 (17 CFR 240.15d-13).", US Securities and Exchange Commission, "Form 10-Q: General Instructions," http://www.sec.gov/about/forms/form10-q.pdf.

information generated by IT systems is what IT does well, but it does get harder. Instead of replacing people, IT is now providing new roles and new methods of obtaining and reporting information to management so that decisions can be based on better information. Management needs to understand and recognize these changes. Adapt its methods and approaches to fiscal pressures by embracing process changes, education, and the migration of existing personnel into roles that leverage their knowledge and experiences. Changing management structures is mere window dressing if the business functions, business rules, and processes are not part of the process. IT is no longer always a method to reduce FTE's. IT enhances what FTE's can do for any organization to increase revenue or reduce the cost of generating revenue.

Chapter Eleven

Data and the Processes That Surround Them

Manufacturing can build the product, management can have strategies and establish goals, marketing can establish the rules and materials used to sell the product, and sales can sell the product, but if you want to measure all of this you need to store data about the process. The process includes more than the basic information of a sale; it is the context that surrounds the data being entered. Surrounding these data are external factors that can provide the context about "why" the sale occurred during this time and at the price paid. Merging these data points will provide the ability to understand reasons the data may present information that varies from other similar data points.

How the data are stored and the relationships established between different data points will determine how effectively the data can feed the classic "data-information-knowledge-wisdom" hierarchy. (See figure 11.1) [51] To generate information, knowledge, and wisdom from data, the data need to have the characteristics of consistent representation of the strategy, business rules, and goals of the organization over time. This concept was outlined in chapter 10. If data are to be used to generate information that then can become knowledge and wisdom, they have to represent these key business aspects so conclusions can be made that have real value. Data are not just generic bits and bytes that anyone can review and extract useful value from. Data are shaped by the reasons they are being collected and retain elements of the macroenvironments in which they are collected. To collect data without some indication of other influential factors that would give context to the data does not acknowledge the changes that take place over time.

When automation of processes and data collection swept into the functional areas of manufacturing, marketing, finance, accounting, sales, nonprofits, and all other areas of business, the collection of information about the quantity wanted, the price to be paid, the customer wanting the product, and what was being purchased were the common data points everyone collected. These data were then summarized, sliced, and diced to extract trends and possible indications of what might happen in the future. All the common ratios used to analyze the financial health and relative equivalency to others doing similar activities were imbedded in the software and reports of automated systems, and all of these advancements and standardizations have established the baseline of data used to create information. The creation of a baseline commoditizes the data used to understand the basics about an organization and its financial health. To create knowledge and wisdom from the data and information, it is necessary

---

[51]   Russell Lincoln Ackoff (12 February 1919 – 29 October 2009) was an American organizational theorist, consultant, and Anheuser-Busch Professor Emeritus of Management Science at the Wharton School, University of Pennsylvania. Ackoff was a pioneer in the field of operations research, systems thinking and management science.Data-Information-Knowledge-Wisdom. "Russel L. Ackoff," http://en.wikipedia.org/wiki/Russell_Lincoln_Ackoff

to understand more about the relationship of the data to the factors that influenced their creation.

An example would be the establishment of a sales incentive program to increase the sales of product X over the next six months. The program included additional commissions being paid and bonuses being given to the top ten salespeople. When the sales of product X increased substantially for six months and then fell off to a historically lower level than before the program was started, everyone knew why and understood the apparent aberration of the sales numbers.

Two years later, a new group of individuals are analyzing historical trends, trying to establish a marketing program for a product to replace product X. Some of the people who knew of the incentive program have left; others have just forgotten about it. There is some documentation of the program and related impacts, but it is not apparent to the individuals analyzing the trends. The missing data are those pertaining to the existence of the sales promotion for the product during the six-month period. If the time frame and sales promotion were also associated with product X, the separate pieces of data would exist for the individuals now trying to extract information, knowledge, and wisdom from these data points.

The existence of the sales promotion and the period of time that it covered are important pieces of data that give context to the sales data for that time frame. Together, these data points provide much better context, and the information generated can create useful knowledge—and perhaps even wisdom. There are many more important data points that could provide context for the sales of this organization. The existence of an economic recession, a significant change in the commodities used to create product X, the generation of an article about the superior nature of product X compared to products from competitors, and fluctuations in currency rates. The conscious decision to collect these data points in a manner that would allow them to be concurrently referenced with the basic sales data of product X would require management and the information technology (IT) department to agree to spend time and resources linking these data points and know that the benefit would be greatest in the future, when the data are retrospectively analyzed. It is unlikely that IT would organize or store these data points without a clear path for utilization by the organization. Having IT push data-collection requirements to management is not common. The storage of information about such things as sales programs could be retrospectively added, but it would be more efficient to create the capability and store the data points in a concurrent manner. These additional layers of data points would allow for a more granular analysis of any organization and the true nature of its business. There are, of course, the additional influences of age demographics, disposable income, and other trends that could be added to the mix of data points needed to create information, knowledge, and wisdom. An argument could be made that there are too many data points added to the mix and that noise would be added to what could be clarity. This brings us to the role of analytics and statistical analysis. Finding the data points that have correlation and focusing on these in future analysis is the end game, and requires you to have the data points.

The need to record data accurately and store them effectively for internal utilization is the standard method established by enterprise resource planning (ERP) systems and all other computerized systems I have utilized. The imbedded nature of these standard methods have caused them to become the inherent blinders that are designed to look inward but not from the outside in. Reversing the lens and now looking into your organization from the perspective of your customers presents one of the great opportunities and risks for your organization. In many ways, the advent of social media is the acknowledgment that the data points outside the organization are relevant and have impact on its internal data points. Having achieved accurate collection of data points opens the opportunity of turning this into an asset for your customers. Linking your organization to your customer in this manner is an excellent marketing tool and achieves one of the holy grails of business: bringing your organization and your customers into a more linked relationship.

I have always considered the opening of FedEx's internal tracking information to the consumers of its services to be brilliant. It reduces the need for customers to contact a person and enables them to determine the status of their delivery. It is now considered a standard of operation, but it leverages one vital aspect of FedEx's business — accurate data. FedEx must have accurate data to deliver the value of its service; determining that its data provided excellent internal value allowed the company to grant data access to its external customers. Can you image giving your vendors access to your accounts payable data? Would the information be organized and accurate enough to give your vendors access so that they could track the status of their bills and payments? If not, what decisions are based on these data, and how good are those decisions? The accounts payable data must be good enough to allow management of bills and payments. But is poor cash flow causing bills to be paid over extended periods of time, and would analysis of payments take into account the relationship to cash on the balance sheet?[52]

The intent is not to associate accurate data with a good cash flow or to place so much value on accurate data that other aspects of the business are ignored or undervalued. The intent is instead to present a philosophy about what expectations are established and what benefits can be derived. The analysis and value of downstream processes and information will be directly related to the accuracy of information at the point of origin. If a chain is as strong as its weakest link, then organizational data cannot be stronger than the accuracy of the original data.

ERP systems that capture vast amounts of data were designed primarily with an internal view of the organization. Internal analysis creates views of how internal processes run, how well

---

52   "In financial accounting, a balance sheet or statement of financial position is a summary of the financial balances of a sole proprietorship, a business partnership, a corporation or other business organization, such as an LLC or an LLP." Wikipedia, "Balance sheet," http://en.wikipedia.org/wiki/Balance_sheet

marketing is presenting products, and how much it costs to generate sales. This improves productivity and provides better data points that can be associated and analyzed but, as with all systems developed in the past, the new processing power and the ability to more cost-effectively store data allows these data to be "crunched" and presented in ways not known ten years ago. This is why there are not standard methods of storing the "context" data to give standard internal data more meaning. Chapter 12 will provide an example of how data and context can be stored and then analyzed. It will also show techniques that can allow data to be valuable for many years into the future.

Figure 11.1. Data-Information-Knowledge-Wisdom

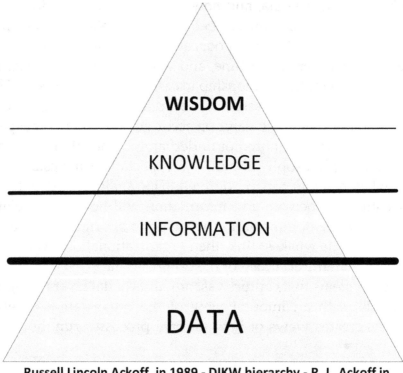

Russell Lincoln Ackoff, in 1989 - DIKW hierarchy - R. L. Ackoff in 1988 - Data-Information-Knowledge-Wisdom.

Fonts of words and lines modified for emphasis.

Chapter Twelve

The Ideal Data Structure Model

There is a common set of criteria that determines if the interface between a human and a computer is successful and the output useful. These criteria are not determined by the kind of software or hardware utilized but by the ability to correctly guide a person to enter the correct data, allow the person to know that the data entered are correct, and save all the information needed to analyze the data in a meaningful manner. You do not need to be a programmer, database administrator, or an expert in information technology (IT) to understand these principles and ask that they be implemented in any software utilized. These concepts would not normally be applied to free-form software like Microsoft Excel, but you can always structure the data in a logical manner. This process and structure is more likely applied for any interface that requires someone to make choices and save those choices so that other actions can be taken.

These concepts will provide flexibility and control over how data are entered, processed, changed, and then presented in some fashion. Data have value if captured accurately and the context around the data is also captured and can then be linked to the data in a meaningful manner. The days of collecting and viewing data from only an internal point of view has passed. If structured systems collect only internal data and not the business rules or external context associated with such data, then the value of the data becomes limited. More effort and thought is required to build this type of structure and to continue to maintain it over time. One aspect of IT is that short-term solutions are developed and limited effort exerted to maintain structures and disciplined approaches to solutions. This is often done because the request is presented as an urgent matter and characterized as a short-term solution that could be corrected or updated in the future. An analogy would be how potholes on busy roadways are addressed in cities. A pothole forms and some asphalt is thrown into the hole and matted down. Everyone knows that it will not last very long or survive a cold snap, but one day a much larger resurfacing project will correct the problem. This logic works for roads, but highly integrated software and data are expensive and too resource intensive to completely rework and modify.

The pain of replacing legacy software and moving to new software and processes was experienced during the mass updates caused by the year 2000. Many programmers had originally written code that did not allow for the calendar to reach the year 2000, and thus that code needed to be modified or replaced. It is unlikely that this scale of change will again be forced upon businesses and organizations in the immediate future, but extending the useful life of these substantial investments would be beneficial, and having quality data that could be migrated to new systems would be excellent. The concept of short-term software fixes and patches should be eliminated. There is a good or bad method of modifying a highly integrated software system such as an ERP system. Information technology is not the real issue to address. It is management's relationship with IT that needs modification. If the quality of IT is based on the IT department's willingness to quickly address issues presented by management, the result will be quick fixes that do not follow best practices or acknowledge the fact that there will never be time to go back and change a quick fix into a thoughtful and thoroughly fleshed-out solution. The concepts of quick fixes date back to a time when IT was much more department-based and the interdependencies of software were not as pervasive. The strong linkages that exist between software and processes also make the concept of quick fixes invalid. As with software, processes no longer have quick fixes available. The impact of changes on any step in a process that has up- and downstream linkages requires assessment before implementation. Frequently the interdependencies of software and processes are not transparent enough for impact analysis. If you can accept the concept of software and processes in an enterprise being so interdependent that they should be thought of as one entity, then the purpose and need for the structures that follow will have a more substantial meaning. In the afterword to this book I will discuss binding software and process in terms of software designed to make process transparent and the linkages interpretable. The structures I will outline can prevent the hard-coding that makes business rules invisible and impact analysis very difficult.

A simple example of how data need to be evaluated and thoroughly considered before building and implementing software and processes provides an example that can be extrapolated to many other data points in any software system. The investment made in establishing these structures correctly will pay dividends for years to come and give users the ability to maintain the structures for current and future needs. Others may not share my belief that software has a life and purpose equivalent to any strategy, product, or investment. The most important benefit from building structures in a forward-thinking manner is flexibility. The ability to adapt more quickly and generate analysis with minimal effort will only present itself when change and events occur over time. It is at this time that the benefits will be understood and generated. It is also very likely that management will not realize that it is benefiting from decisions and actions taken in the past so these decisions and actions need to be imbedded in strategy statements and presented correctly before the benefits can be fully experienced.

Postal codes are a simple example. They are not a topic of great interest for many, but they are a classic example of something every company and software package utilizes. The very first classic mistake that small companies make early in their existence is not thinking globally. If the Internet has done nothing else, it has made every business capable of being international. This one realization should affect how software and data are first structured and how they are structured for the future.

Postal codes in United States and Canada differ in their structure. These differences should impact how postal codes are entered, validated, and used in business reporting. Getting the correct value entered is step 1, but having the structure established comes *before* step 1.

In the United States, the first digit in a zip code represents a certain group of states; the second and third digits represent a region in that group (or a large city). The fourth and fifth digits represent a group of delivery addresses within that region. In 1983, the US Postal Service began using an expanded zip code system called "ZIP + 4", also known as "plus-four codes" or "add-on codes."

In Canada, the postal code follows the format *letter-number-letter (space) number-letter-number*. The first three characters are called the forward sortation area (FSA); the last three characters are called the local delivery unit (LDU).

The first letter in the FSA represents one of eighteen regions in Canada. The number is a zero for a rural area, and any other digit for an urban area. The second letter represents a specific rural region, entire medium-size city, or section of a major metropolitan area.

The LDU represents a specific single address or range of addresses, which can correspond to an entire small town, a significant part of a medium-size town, a single side of a city block in larger cities, a single large building or a portion of a very large one, a single large institution such as a university or a hospital, or a business that receives large volumes of mail on a regular basis.

LDUs ending in zero correspond to postal facilities, from post offices and small drugstore retail postal outlets all the way up to sortation plants. In urban areas, LDUs may be specific postal carriers' routes. In rural areas where direct door-to-door delivery is not available, an LDU can describe a set of post office boxes or a rural route.

This very simple example shows the amount of information imbedded in the fundamental data known as postal codes. Integrating these data with census, marketing, and demographic data of all types is common and useful.

The first step is to build a structure that will contain customer information, which will contain postal code information.

A limited value structure could look like top portion of table 12.1.

Table 12.1 The Ideal Data Model

Data Element Name	Data Value	Defined As	Length	Rule	Linked To
Table Key	100	Number	8	Must be number; max 8	Nothing
Name	JOHN ADAMS	Alphanumeric	30	Max 30	Nothing
Street Line One	123 Washington Blvd.	Alphanumeric	30	Max 30	Nothing
Street Line Two		Alphanumeric	30	Max 30	Nothing
State	DE	Alphanumeric	2	Max 2	Nothing
Zip Code	65432	Alphanumeric	10	Max 10	Nothing
Country		Alphanumeric	3	Max 30	Nothing

A more effective structure would look like the following.

Data Elment Name	Data Value	Defined As	Length	Rule	Linked To
Table Key	10000000016	Number	11	Must be number; Force length 11	Nothing
First Name	JOHN	Alphanumeric	25	Must be entered; Force uppercase; Max 30	Nothing
Last Name	ADAMS	Alphanumeric	30	Must be entered; Force uppercase; Max 30	Nothing
Middle Intial		Alphanumeric	1	Max 1; Force uppercase;	Nothing
Surname(s)		Alphanumeric	40	Force uppercase	
Country	USA	Alphanumeric	3	Must be valid Country Code	To COUNTRY CODE table
Street Line One	123 ELM BLVD.	Alphanumeric	40	Must be entered; Force uppercase; Max 40	Nothing
Stree Line Two		Alphanumeric	40	Max 40; if entered, Force uppercase	Nothing
Message Line		Alphanumeric	40	Max 40; if entered, Force uppercase	Nothing
State	DE	Alphanumeric	2	Must be entered; Must be valid State Code; Entry determined by Country	To STATE CODE table
Postal Code USA	65432	Number	5	Must be entered; must be 5 numbers; Entry determined by Country	To VALID USA POSTAL CODE table
Postal Code US Last Four	0000	Number	4	Must be 4 numbers; Entry determined by Country	To VALID USA POSTAL 4 CODE table
Provincial Code CAD		Alphanumeric	2	Canadian subnational postal; Entry determined by Country	To VALID CAD Subnational Postal table
Provincial Postal Code CAD		Alphanumeric	6	Must be valid Provincial Code; Force uppercase; must be 6 characters; Entry determined by Country	To VALID CAD POSTAL CODE table
Manual Code	XYZ-12345	Alphanumeric	40	Max 40; if entered, Force uppercase; Entry determined by Country	
Parent Number	10000000100	Number	11	Must be an existing value; Must be number; Force length 11	To CUSTOMER table (itself)

There are number of aspects, in the second part, that require identification and explanation.

The *table key*, which is the unique identifier for this one record, is a large number that allows for growth and the use of a check digit.[53] After you have written ten or more reports, you realize that the numbers of values in any table will continue to grow over time, but you may only be seeing the smaller version of the number. So consumers and report writers do not suffer from limiting the size of customer identification codes because of increasing size; start with a large number that will last a long time and allow for growth. Having the same number of digits for all customer identification codes is also of benefit when sorting information. The check digit ensures that the entry of customer numbers in all other processes will not accidentally be the incorrect value if it is manually entered. Ensuring that the correct customer number is identified is first on the list of tasks to always execute correctly.

All *alphanumeric* values are uppercase. Having the system automatically convert values to uppercase is an easy and logical method of having consistent presentation of data on screens and in reports. All larger databases allow for the conversion of case, on alphanumeric values, to upper- and lowercase. No one will notice this standard unless it is not followed. It is not until people start to see a mixed collection of cases that people realize there is no standard.

Determining which data values require their own unique value is critical. Splitting up the name into first and last is obvious to many. It becomes less obvious with the middle initial, foreign surnames,[54] and titles. Marketing will likely view access to this

---

53   "A check digit is a form of redundancy check used for error detection, the decimal equivalent of a binary checksum. It consists of a single digit computed from the other digits in the message. With a check digit, one can detect simple errors in the input of a series of digits, such as a single mistyped digit or some permutations of two successive digits." Wikipedia, "Check digit," http://en.wikipedia.org/wiki/Check_digit

54   "In Spain and in most Spanish-speaking countries, the custom is for people to have two surnames. Usually the first surname comes from the father and the second from the mother, but it could be the other way round. A child's first surname will usually be their father's first surname whilst the child's second surname will usually be the mother's first surname." Wikipedia, "Surname – Spanish compound surnames," http://en.wikipedia.org/wiki/Surnames

type of information more highly than will accounting. As I have learned, it is common for Spanish names to have two surnames. If you are going to think in terms of the world, then make sure your software does not force an American view of the world on all countries. I am not covering other topics like Unicode,[55], but you should at least be aware that there are other factors to consider.

Country codes are vital and need to be correct. Having an additional table that contains validated codes and using it to validate the entry of country codes in all screens is easy, logical, and should not be thought of as optional. Having only validated values in these types of code fields will benefit all report writers and users of the data in the table. It also should force a discussion about how customers' identification should be entered. Customers who have locations in multiple countries require a parent-child relationship to be created. There are many reasons you may need to break one customer into several values, and your own business processes will provide guidance. You can also store other values that are country-specific in the country code part of the table—perhaps currency codes, language codes, or anything else you may believe could be of value. The key point is that the value is determined, and used to guarantee what data are entered into a field.

Having *street lines* is common, but reserving room for a *message line* is less so. You may find that you want to communicate additional information like "attention of" or something you do not yet know. You may be told not to waste disk space with mostly empty fields, or that the additional work has no tangible benefit based on the current business model. I am a big believer in the simple fact that everything changes. Just like business strategies, thinking about how things may change will pay off in the long run.

The *state codes* are like the *country codes*. They are known and need to be validated. This example has a *provincial code* as a separate data value, as well as a *manual code*. Canada has a known

---

55   "Unicode is a computing industry standard for the consistent encoding, representation and handling of text expressed in most of the world's writing systems." Wikipedia, "Unicode," http://en.wikipedia.org/wiki/Unicode

set of provincial codes, and these can be predefined. The *country code* can be used by the software to require only the code that is correct so that the user does not have to make the determination. That is, the country code "CA" will require a *provincial code* and bypass the *state code*. If, for example, an African country did not have codes that you could predetermine, the *manual code* would then be used to meet this need. Validate what you can, and allow for those things you cannot validate as a separate value. The key is that the software and table structures determine what is valid based on business rules that use data in tables. People who communicate with customers need to focus on the customer and the conversation taking place, not on remembering which fields should be entered based on the country of the customer. This requires more effort for those creating the software and table structures, but no one would challenge the need of a house to have a foundation that supported the design and functionality desired in the upper floors. Unfortunately, management and users will not fully appreciate or understand the magnitude of the benefits until they experience their absence. I am not saying you need to force an organization to use badly structured software and data so that it understands such value; there have been enough failed IT systems written about and the causes of the failures explained in great detail. This is the educational requirement IT must assume and execute along with implementation. Fear is a strong force. The "I've fallen and I can't get up" TV commercial is based on invoking fear about what could happen to someone in his or her own home. You need to find a way to take this example and make it tangible for consumption by your organization. There is a real and tangible cost and impact of taking the lazy way out of software and data development.

This very basic example presents the philosophy I have about data entry and table structures. It requires discipline and a sense of pride in the piece of the organization that you affect. My experiences with outsourced software development and consultant-driven development have shown that applying this type of philosophy is difficult. As mentioned previously, if you believe you are in a commodity environment and you can leverage canned software and table structures to limit the cost side of your business, then go for it. If this is not true, place the correct balance of value and strategy on the IT segment of the business.

There is one aspect I have not addressed directly — that of *context*. As I write this, the hot concept is "big data," which includes things like unstructured data[56]. Social media generally comprises unstructured data, and requires a different approach to provide context to data that are collected within a time frame associated with the data. There are numerous articles and books being written on this topic, and I present the topic here because some basic context could be added to data from unstructured data. One of the basic facets of social media is the concept of positive, neutral, or negative trends existing during the period the data are collected, which could be daily, weekly, or monthly. Basically, a data field could exist that indicates that this day, week, or month was positive, neutral, or negative, and then correlated with the expenses, revenue, or profit generated during that period of time. This is a very basic example, but it presents the concept of context from outside the organization being associated with data monitored internally by the organization.

The data field could be called "Social Media" and have a value of 1 = positive, 0 = neutral, and -1 = negative. This is also called sentiment analysis. If summed over any period of time, the amount of profit for a year could be associated with how positive, neutral, or negative social media was during this time frame. I previously mentioned context related to sales promotions. There could be two date fields that are associated with a product code to indicate the start and end period. Also, text or a code that indicates a sales promotion to facilitate analysis.

---

56   "Unstructured Data (or unstructured information) refers to information that either does not have a pre-defined data model and/or does not fit well into relational tables. Unstructured information is typically text-heavy, but may contain data such as dates, numbers, and facts as well." Wikipedia, "Unstructured data," http://en.wikipedia.org/wiki/Unstructured_data

Table 12.2. The Context Data Model

CONTEXT DATA

		Rule	Linked To	Report
Social Media Trend Date	Date	Must be valid date	Nothing	Can be selected and used as a range
Social Media Trend Value	Number	Must be number of 1,0,-1	Nothing	Can be summed
Sales Promotion Product	Alpha Numeric	Must be entered, Force upper case, Max 30	Product Table	Can Be Selected and filtered
Sales promotion Start Date	Date	Must be valid date	Nothing	Can be selected and used as a range
Sales Promotion End Date	Date	Must be valid date and equal or larger than Start Date	Nothing	Can be selected and used as a range

The demands placed on IT now and in the future will not diminish, nor will IT's strategic value lessen. Individuals working within IT are often cross-trained in the functional area in which they operate and in the IT functions they provide. The greater the exposure to various functional areas of the organization, the more potential understanding of how to link and cross-pollinate the IT data and tools for end users. This value can be leveraged strategically or viewed as a good support plan. Not every individual working in IT can or wants to become more integrated into strategy and interwoven into functional processes, but the path—for those that can and want to achieve objectives—needs to exist and be acknowledged. Those who recognize and leverage all the assets they possess will benefit more over time than those who do not. Director John Woo's 2003 film *Paycheck* is about someone who creates a machine that can look into the future and sees that he will die unless he follows a very specific plan. Unfortunately, part of his job agreement is to wipe his memories about his work out of his mind. He leaves himself an envelope with objects that will allow him to go back and stop these events, but he must figure out how to use each item as he finds himself in various precarious situations.

Objects of no apparent value become objects that save his life. It is all about finding and understanding value and using it in a beneficial manner.

Afterword: Process

I have outlined my view of how process is integrated, interwoven, and dependent on information technology (IT) functions and the need for transparency of the business rules imbedded. I have been in search of a tool that would provide these necessary capabilities to an organization by just existing. I have recently read about smart process applications.[57] Forrester has introduced the concept of "software design principles that are created for people and built for change":

> Most business applications are too inflexible to keep pace with the businesses they support. Today's applications force people to figure out how to map isolated pools of information and functions to their tasks and processes, and they force IT pros to spend too much budget to keep up with evolving markets, policies, regulations, and business models. IT's primary goal during the next five years should be to invent a new generation of enterprise software that adapts to the business and its work and evolves with it. Forrester calls this new generation Dynamic Business Applications, emphasizing close alignment with business processes and work (design for people) and adaptability to business change (build for change). *At this stage, the requirements for Dynamic Business Applications are clearer than the design practices needed to create them.*[58]

---

57   See Andrew Bartels and Connie Moore, "The Next Frontier for Software: Smart Process Applications Fill a Big Gap," http://www.kmworld.com/Articles/Editorial/Features/The-next-frontier-for-software-Smart-process-applications-fill-a-big-gap-85806.aspx.

58   John R. Rymer and Connie Moore with Tom Pohlmann, Mike Gilpin, Sharyn Leaver, Catherine Salzinger, and Katie Smillie, *The Dynamic Business Applications Imperative—A Client Choice Report*, http://www.forrester.com/The+Dynamic+Business+Applications+Imperative/fulltext/-/E-RES41397.

Vertically oriented smart process applications that will be built on Business Process Management (BPM) platforms. Just as traditional application vendors have built smart process application extensions of their core systems, vertical application vendors, such as Siemens (siemens.com) in hospital management systems, have built industry-specific custom applications. This segment has explosive growth potential as vendors and individual companies realize that applications created for a singular firm have relevance to many others in the same industry"[59]

Dynamic business applications or vertically oriented smart process applications are concepts that have some overlap with the topics covered in this book. For enterprise software to adapt to a business and evolve with that business it must be clear what needs to be accomplished; I would call it dynamic process management, because the understanding of the process and the changing of the process must be transparent and visual. It is interesting to see the concept of vertically integrated and targeted software being the solution to issues presented by today's standardized software packages; time will determine if these approaches are in fact the next generation of software. The approach also implies that these software packages will interact with businesses that have common processes and execution methodologies. I do not know if this pushes the very same businesses into a common set of processes and procedures that make them a commodity instead of a unique and differentiated business; this will be determined by time and execution. There are other possibilities, and they can leverage the existing infrastructure but involve a more sophisticated process control technology.

I have tried to outline a philosophy for non-IT individuals to use, support, and extract what is wanted and needed from IT. I have studied one product, for several years, that has maintained my interest and that I hope to one day merge with the principles

---

59   Andrew Bartels and Connie Moore, "The Next Frontier."

outlined in this book. My interest is based on the concept of making processes transparent to users and connecting all the functional areas to the processes that are upstream and downstream from the point of interest in a visual and analytical manner.

One of my past jobs was as a director of knowledge management. I really liked the title, as knowledge management was one of those IT trends that sounded sexy. I had to explain to every person who asked what I did for a living that it was not an oxymoron. It was during this time that I first learned of Knowledge Genes (i.e. Why Code) (at the time the name was HyperKnowledge).[60] This software visually maps out the processes of any organization into what, how, and why structures.

"The first questions in increasing productivity - in working smarter - have to be:

WHAT is the task? WHAT do we try to accomplish? WHY do it at all?" - Peter Drucker

"The WHY Code. Everything in this World has a set of fundamental WHY points—reasons for existence. Once these are understood, you can truly focus, innovate and succeed."

Since I am always interested in finding a way to execute my philosophy with tools that benefit IT and the entire organization, I have examined how blending my philosophy and this tool into a model that allows someone to visualize the up- and downstream linkages that exist in any process and data stream. These linkages are based on the *what, how,* and *why* natures of processes. Imagine having a tool that would allow you to link your organizational strategy statements all the way down to the execution of a specific task and allow a person to know how the task supports the company's strategy—a visual path that would allow everyone to understand his or her role within the umbrella of strategy in a clear and precise manner, to clearly understand how a change in

---

60   For more on Knowledge Genes, go to http://www.knowledgegenes.com/welcome.aspx.

one part of a process impacts downstream activities. This may be a method to address the issue brought up in the dynamic business applications quote above: *"At this stage, the requirements for Dynamic Business Applications are clearer than the design practices needed to create them."*

The article "The Curious Case of a Broken Crumb Trail," by Dr. John Lewis of Explanation Age and Art Murray of Applied Knowledge Sciences, outlines a very interesting case of rediscovered research that outlines the benefits of using thorium as a nuclear fuel source. Lewis and Murray explain how these benefits were identified and how they were lost:

> So how did we get to this point? As it turns out, much of our lost knowledge is the result of how we make decisions and how we document them. When we make decisions, we tend to make them serially. Many small decisions build upon one another to the point where momentum often prevails over logic. Once we go down a certain road, it becomes increasingly difficult to back up and regroup as conditions change.
>
> The way we document our decisions is problematic as well. Decision trees, influence diagrams and the like help us visualize and keep track of the factors that go into the "which" surrounding a decision (which fuel, which design, etc.) but fail to capture the "why."[61]

As of right now, I have not convinced any organization to blend these concepts together, but it is one of my "bucket list" goals.

This is not some cheap advertisement. I am pointing to an interesting concept that incorporates ideas that organizations could

---

61   John Lewis and Art Murray, "The Curious Case of a Broken Crumb Trail," http://www.kmworld.com/Articles/Column/The-Future-of-the-Future/The-curious-case-of-a-broken-crumb-trail-87836.aspx.

benefit from in a meaningful manner. If I started a business today, I would make this part of my business model. As with everything I have discussed in this book, it would take time and effort to execute and maintain, but the elimination of the time spent by an organization trying to maintain an understanding of, teach, and relearn their processes would free time to be a smarter organization. This is what intrigues me: building an organization that functions like no other and prospers by melding processes, data, and information technology.

If you are intrigued, investigate. If you are not thinking about what could be, you are working in what is. That is not wrong or bad, but I find that looking forward is a more interesting way of working.

Appendix 1: What Is Controlled Customization?

No data or table structure can predetermine the myriad possible demands that users of data may present over time, but you can create a structure that allows users to own a piece of data attached to some standard data structure, such as information about a customer. The ability to enter one or more text, numeric, or date values into a customer-linked table structure would allow users to aggregate or select information about these customers in some type of reporting format. This kind of data structure could exist for other groups such as the marketing, finance, or service departments. Output reports could then be created that would access these values and allow for selection of some or all values present. The information technology department would not know what the codes mean or what the aggregations represent; this is not the purpose of these values. Instead, they are opportunities for non-IT groups to extract data from existing table structures in a manner that has context for them. Information technology may have created the data fields and report prompts that are used, but not the context in which they are used. If functional groups or individuals are willing to add these data values into established structures, they can test out ideas or theories about customers that are not yet proven or fully understood. These prompt values would be added to existing reports of known functionality that present data about sales and products. If these prompts are selected with other established prompt values, the data or information presented would have these additional attributes and then be available for slicing and dicing in something like a Microsoft Excel pivot table.

Their intended meaning is known by those who entered the data, but not by others. The content is controlled by a known group or individual, but does not impact standard reporting or others in the organization. Some may not have these data entered, or some may have all fields loaded with these types of data elements. The information technology department provided the structures and reports, but the value is determined by those who enter the data. Based on my previous example in chapter 12, these data elements would have support tables containing the valid universe of elements and would be validated against these values.

This is controlled customization. Data are customized by users and analyzed by users, without IT knowing the context. They are controlled, and can be as much or as little as the users desire them to be.

Table A1.1 shows what this might look like.

Table A1.1. Controlled Customization

ROBUST ORGANIZATION DATA ELEMENTS

Data Element Name	Data Value	Defined As	Length	Rule	Linked To
Table Key	10000000016	Number	11	Must be number; Force length 11	Nothing
First Name	JOHN	Alphanumeric	25	Must be entered; Force uppercase; Max 30	Nothing
Last Name	ADAMS	Alphanumeric	30	Must be entered; Force uppercase; Max 30	Nothing
Middle Intial		Alphanumeric	1	Max 1; Force uppercase;	Nothing
Surname(s)		Alphanumeric	40	Force uppercase	
Country	USA	Alphanumeric	3	Must be valid Country Code	To COUNTRY CODE table
Street Line One	123 ELM BLVD.	Alphanumeric	40	Must be entered; Force uppercase; Max 40	Nothing
Stree Line Two		Alphanumeric	40	Max 40; if entered, Force uppercase	Nothing
Message Line		Alphanumeric	40	Max 40; if entered, Force uppercase	Nothing
State	DE	Alphanumeric	2	Must be entered; Must be valid State Code; Entry determined by Country	To STATE CODE table
Postal Code USA	65432	Number	5	Must be entered; must be 5 numbers; Entry determined by Country	To VALID USA POSTAL CODE table
Postal Code US Last Four	0000	Number	4	Must be 4 numbers; Entry determined by Country	To VALID USA POSTAL 4 CODE table
Provincial Code CAD		Alphanumeric	2	Canadian subnational postal; Force uppercase; Entry determined by Country	To VALID CAD Subnational Postal table
Provincial Postal Code CAD		Alphanumeric	6	Must be valid Provincial Code; Force uppercase; must be 6 characters; Entry determined by Country	To VALID CAD POSTAL CODE table
Manual Code	XYZ-12345	Alphanumeric	40	Max 40; if entered, Force uppercase; Entry determined by Country	
Parent Number	10000000100	Number	11	Must be an existing value; Must be number; Force length 11	To CUSTOMER table (itself)

CONTROLLED CUSTOMIZATION

Controlled Customization		Rule	Linked To	Report
Marketing Code 1	Alphanumeric	Must be entered; Force uppercase; Max 30	Custom Table 1 (Code and Description)	Can Be Selected and filtered
Marketing Code 2	Alphanumeric	Must be entered; Force uppercase; Max 30	Custom Table 2 (Code and Description)	Can Be Selected and filtered
Marketing Date 1	Date	Must be valid date or null	Nothing	Can be selected and used as a range
Marketing Date 2	Date	Must be valid date or null	Nothing	Can be selected and used as a range
Marketing Number 1	Number	Must be number; Force length 11	Nothing	Can be selected, summed, filtered, used as a range

	Type	Rule	Linked To	
Marketing Number 2	Number	Must be number; Force length 11	Nothing	Can be selected, summed, filtered, used as a range
Sales Code 1	Alphanumeric	Must be entered; Force uppercase; Max 30	Custom Table 1 (Code and Description)	Can Be Selected and filtered
Sales Code 2	Alphanumeric	Must be entered; Force uppercase; Max 30	Custom Table 2 (Code and Description)	Can Be Selected and filtered
Sales Date 1	Date	Must be valid date or null	Nothing	Can be selected and used as a range
Sales Date 2	Date	Must be valid date or null	Nothing	Can be selected and used as a range
Sales Number 1	Number	Must be number; Force length 11	Nothing	Can be selected, summed, filtered, used as a range
Sales Number 2	Number	Must be number; Force length 11	Nothing	Can be selected, summed, filtered, used as a range
SERVICE VALUES...	Alphanumeric	Must be entered; Force uppercase; Max 30	Custom Table 1 (Code and Description)	Can Be Selected and filtered
FINANCE VALUES...	Alphanumeric	Must be entered; Force uppercase; Max 30	Custom Table 1 (Code and Description)	Can Be Selected and filtered
Other Code 1	Alphanumeric	Must be entered; Force uppercase; Max 30	Custom Table 1 (Code and Description)	Can Be Selected and filtered
Other Code 2	Alphanumeric	Must be entered; Force uppercase; Max 30	Custom Table 2 (Code and Description)	Can Be Selected and filtered
Other Date 1	Date	Must be valid date or null	Nothing	Can Be Selected and filtered
Other Date 2	Date	Must be valid date or null	Nothing	Can be selected and used as a range
Other Number 1	Number	Must be number; Force length 11	Nothing	Can be selected, summed, filtered, used as a range
Other Number 2	Number	Must be number; Force length 11	Nothing	Can be selected, summed, filtered, used as a range

CONTEXT DATA

		Rule	Linked To	Report
Social Media Trend Date	Date	Must be valid date	Nothing	Can be selected and used as a range
Social Media Trend Value	Number	Must be number of 1, 0, -1	Nothing	Can be summed
Sales Promotion Product	Alphanumeric	Must be entered; Force uppercase; Max 30	Product Table	Can Be Selected and filtered
Sales Promotion Start Date	Date	Must be valid date	Nothing	Can be selected and used as a range
Sales Promotion End Date	Date	Must be valid date and equal or larger than Start Date	Nothing	Can be selected and used as a range

A report may have these type of prompts established:

{These are the standard prompts for the organization}

Note: <u>Must enter one type of date</u>

Start Date Range : [*start date*]   - - Invoice date entered or leave blank for all

Ending Date Range: [*end date*]   - - Invoice date entered or leave blank for all

Date: [*date*] [G or L]   - - Invoice date or leave blank for all
(G)reater than or (L)ess than this Date

Customer Number(s):   - - Customer number(s) or leave blank for all
[*number 1, number 2, etc.*]

Sales Territorie(s):   - - Territory/territories) or leave blank for all
[*territory 1, territory 2, etc.*]

{Controlled Customization Prompts}

Start Date Range : [*start date*]   - - Marketing date one entered or leave blank for all

Ending Date Range: [*end date*]   - - Marketing date two entered or leave blank for all

Date: [*marketing date one*] [G or L]   - - Marketing date one or leave blank for all
(G)reater than or (L)ess than this Date

Marketing Code(s) One: - - Marketing code or leave blank for all
[code 1, code 2, etc.] [I or E] (I)ncluded or (E)xcluded

Marketing Codes between: - - Marketing codes or leave blank
[code 1] and [code 2]

Marketing Number(s) One: [marketing number 1, marketing number 2, etc.]
[I or E] (I)ncluded or (E)xcluded   - - Enter or leave blank for all

Marketing Number between: - - Enter or leave blank for all
[marketing number 1] and [marketing number 2]

Fields for Sales, Service, Finance, and Other would follow.

Appendix 2: What Consultants Bring to the Table

—⟪⟫—

This is from an article I wrote and published in *ADVANCE for Health Information Executives*, February 1, 1998.

> *I am inserting this older article to highlight some of my previous thoughts and show how they have evolved. It also addresses some of the concepts covered in chapter 9 from a different perspective.*

When an organization decides to use a consulting group, it can be faced with two courses of action. Either the consultant leads the organization on a clear, definitive, and productive path to the goal or it leaves the organization empty and no closer to its objective.

Organizations that want to embark on a new direction, process, plan or methodology need to understand that consultants bring both strengths and weaknesses to the table. These must be understood and balanced with the organization's resources and objectives. Understanding these issues and knowing how to evaluate consulting group services increases the odds of achieving the project's objectives and receiving the organization's support.

Using consultants

We will first look at the strengths a consultant brings to a project. A consultant usually utilizes some type of process or methodology that provides a structure for the duration of the project and ensures that all work is completed. Often, this process or methodology is documented and follows a workflow pattern that needs further explanation.

Understanding how much time is required to create the project deliverables (versus obtaining the information for the deliverables) is necessary and allows for personnel resources to be allocated solely for the creation process.

Keep in mind that consultants provide objectivity, which is essential to the successful completion of any project that changes or challenges existing processes or an organization's structure. The organization's internal politics can be minimized or even by-passed if senior management supports the purpose and need for the project. A consultant draws on past experiences and the strength of a process or methodology to ensure that the outcome is positive despite the organization's inherent resistance to change.

Consultants also provide knowledge and resources that most businesses do not have the time or ability to develop. In addition consultants provide an understanding of where the organization stands in relation to similar organizations. All parties must know how this information will be presented and how it relates to the project. Of course, the organization then becomes part of the consultant's knowledge base.

On the other hand, consultants have their weaknesses. Consultants want to generate revenue for themselves and their organization. Sometimes a project may be underpriced or the time to complete the project underestimated in the hope of generating additional work from the project or from a spin-off project. The consultant may then become involved in the internal politics of the organization that may actually lead to some difficult issues being downplayed or avoided. The IT executive should clearly state that these issues are understood and that your organization will not tolerate manipulation of projects.

Further, consultants may be inflexible because of the internal politics within their own organization; they may want to make their process or methodology generic, or they may want to promote the belief that all organizations can benefit from their type of change. Your organization must be aware of this possible issue and make sure team members do not blindly follow the consultant's lead.

At several points throughout the project, take time to review and make any necessary adjustments. Identifying these intermediate points from the start will help both the organization and the consultant maintain an awareness that evaluations will be conducted throughout the project. It's extremely rare to find a perfect blending of talents or personalities in any team, but clearly understood rules and objectives allow the project to move forward and minimize the negatives.

Consultants must consistently communicate to management, the team members and other members of the organization and not alter the message to meet the needs of the audience. Inconsistent communication creates distrust and confusion, and gives rise for the need for additional communication. If someone on the team identifies poor or improper communication, it needs to be promptly addressed and corrected. It's important for both parties to constantly monitor the team's communication, because of the role it plays in the successful completion of the project.

If other projects are already underway, internal resources may be used by more than one project group. This is not a concern if each project addresses different issues. But if a new project overlaps with an existing project, adjustments need to be made to avoid duplicating efforts, personnel time and deliverables.

Internal resources

The role your resources play in the project must be defined and understood by all parties. From the beginning, identify how much time is needed, what other projects might be affected and how much time will be spent on the new project.

You cannot prevent conflicts or issues from arising during a project, but the way in which they are addressed and resolved must be identified and understood by all parties. If the organization does not allow time for existing team member activities, then team members will be unable to devote themselves entirely to the project.

Often, a large project relies heavily on the organization's best personnel resources. Identify team members' personnel growth objectives and compare them to the project plan. If there are mismatches, discuss them and come to a resolution.

It is important to provide knowledge growth, skill improvements, and "cross-pollination" opportunities for various corporate processes, business rules and information sources. If the project supports the needs of the individual and the organization, a win-win situation develops. Personnel resources are the largest investment of an organization and by blending individual and organizational objectives, the organization receives the greatest return on investment.

Before the start of a project, the team may need to develop similar skill sets to produce the defined deliverables. It is vital that examples of the work being performed be given and that the skill sets of each team member be compared to the skills outlined in the sample work.

It may be impossible to establish a common skill set for everyone in the group, but the methodology for working through any skill level issue should be outlined and integrated into the project's time line.

The project group's management structure should be balanced between outside and internal resources. The organization should also understand the consulting group's management structure. This will help your personnel to understand how and why the consultant has done certain things or taken certain actions.

The organization also needs a management group that evaluates the end result. A senior executive is often designated to regularly work with the project team leader. However, it is important that the senior executive and the project leader not directly report to each other. Established communication pathways can cause issues to not be addressed because of existing understandings.

New communication pathways allow fresh views to be interjected into the process and a new organizational relationship to develop.

Final product
All parties must know what the final product is going to be, identify what the end result should look like and discuss what issues might come up during the project. It is always easier to understand the final goal if examples are given.

Additionally, the consulting group and the organization must identify the life span of the project. If this is not specified, an organization's daily operations may cause the project to falter or fail. The organization may develop "consultant fatigue," forcing each new project team to overcome a set of residual issues from past projects before they can become productive.

Project success
Once your organization decides to use a consultant, follow these preliminary steps before making any recommendations to management.

First, designate an expert for every area of corporate activity; the expert may have worked for a consulting firm, in academia or may have published articles in books or magazines. If you don't have a resident expert, the Internet, local library or bookstore are good places to begin to get a perspective on the topic. This preliminary work is effective in introducing senior management to the issues and ideas associated with the project.

This research will provide insight that helps the organization select a consultant. Ultimately, the individuals executing the project determine what needs to be accomplished. But having clearly defined roles, objectives and methods gives any project the best chance for success.

THE END

"I see," said the blind man as he walked into the valley of death.

This is a saying I have said so many times that my daughters just roll their eyes when they hear it. It is a blend of a phrase from Alfred, Lord Tennyson's poem "The Charge of the Light Brigade" and Psalm 23:4. I may have it heard said once, but do not remember when or where. I just wanted to get it into the book.

INDEX

www.ingramcontent.com/pod-product-compliance
Lightning Source LLC
Chambersburg PA
CBHW071203050326
40689CB00011B/2230